YOU CAN HAVE VICTORY

Living the Victorious Christian Life

by
Rev. Gary A. Mitrik

Gary Mitrik/Greater Works Outreach
301 College Park Drive
Monroeville, Pennsylvania 15146
(412) 327-6500

Editorial Assistance by Stephen R. Clark.
Unless otherwise specified, all Scripture quotations
are from the New King James Version.

Foreword

It is said, "Show me a man's companions and I'll tell you what kind of a man he is."

Proverbs says, "A mirror reflects a man's face, but what he is really like is shown by the kinds of friends he chooses."

Friendship is developed. It begins with an introduction, then an acquaintanceship followed by fellowship, companionship and eventually it can lead to friendship.

Basic friendship is predicated on truth.

Truth is always trustworthy. So are real friends.

Friends are life's greatest treasure.

They are the wealth of life.

Books containing the truth's of God's kingdom are a treasure in life, and can be a man's best friend, and give him his greatest companionship.

Finding such books are like discovering a pearl in an oyster, a diamond in a coal bin, or a friend among strangers.

Gary Mitrik has written such a book.

His exhortation to live on new levels of faith, to enjoy a life of spiritual achievement, and to walk as God intended us to — make this book something that can become a friend for life.

He has given us truths we can trust.

You Can Have Victory is more than a book title, it is a way of life that Gary Mitrik shares with us to enhance our life. Enjoy it.

Contents

Introduction

Searching for Excellence

Everyone today is searching for excellence. Businesses are looking for more excellent ways to do business. Career people are looking for more excellent careers. Christian teachers are trying to present a more excellent Gospel. And Christians are trying to discern the most excellent way to achieve success in life!

I'm sure you want excellence in your Christian life, too. Don't we all? But, what is God's excellence?

The Psalmist mentioned God's excellence several times: "O Lord, our Lord, How excellent is Your name in all the earth" (Psalm 8:1, 9); "You are more glorious and excellent than the mountains of prey" (76:4); "Let them praise the name of the Lord, For His name alone is exalted [excellent]" (148:13); "Praise Him according to His excellent greatness!" (150:2).

It's easy to see what is meant by God's excellence. He is our Creator, and everything He is and does is excellent. It's good. It's perfect. It's complete.

But what about excellence in the Christian life? Can you and I achieve excellence? Again, the Psalmist provides insight.

Keep and protect me, O God, for in You I have found refuge, and in You do I put my trust and hide myself.

I say to the Lord, You are my Lord; I have no good beside or beyond You.

As for the godly (the saints) who are in the land, they are the excellent, the noble, and the glorious, in whom is all my delight (Psalm 16:1-3, Amplified Bible).

David is expressing his dependency upon God, and states how he enjoys the fellowship of others who are believers (saints). He refers to these who share his belief in and obedience to God as the excellent, the noble, the glorious.

I believe this is the spiritual standard God wants us to match our Christian walk to.

Excellence indicates perfection or completion. Hebrews 13:21 says, "[May God] make you complete [perfect] in every good work to do His will, working in you what is well pleasing in His sight, through Jesus Christ, to whom be glory forever and ever. Amen." And even Christ commanded that we "be perfect, just as your Father in heaven is perfect" (Matthew 5:48).

Do you feel perfect in your faith? That's what you're

called to! In Christ, you're also an heir to nobility.

Jesus Christ is the Lord of lords and the King of kings. Galatians 3:29 states, "if you are Christ's, then you are . . . heirs according to the promise." Being born again means being born of God, which means being born of spiritual nobility!

And finally, David refers to Christians as being "glorious." As a believer you are part of the body of Christ — His Church. Ephesians 5:25-27 states, "Christ . . . loved the church and gave Himself for it, that He might sanctify and cleanse it with the washing of water by the word, that He might present it to Himself a glorious church, not having spot or wrinkle or any such thing, but that it should be holy and without blemish."

I believe you are called to godly excellence, or, a victorious Christian life. And this book is aimed at showing you how to attain victory, God's excellence.

If you're looking for easy answers and instant solutions, you'll not find them here. Nor will you discover God's excellence or achieve spiritual victory without paying the price of committed discipleship.

Excellence in any walk of life doesn't come without effort and perseverance. The same is true for Christians. Victory doesn't come cheaply. Yet, it does come.

When you accepted Christ as your personal Savior, God opened to you all the resources you need to step into victorious living. The potential for victory in your life is real. But just as the children of Israel had to possess their Promised Land once they reached it, so you too have to possess your victory in the Lord.

Do you want God's excellence? Do you want a victorious Christian walk? Then, read on. I want to show you how to possess the victory that is yours in Christ Jesus.

CHAPTER ONE

Victory in the Word

In this modern and fast-paced world, it's so easy to become confused by the many voices, each claiming to have "the" right answer. Self-made gurus and so-called spiritual leaders abound, all clamoring for your attention. Yet, do they really have the answers? No. There is only one source of truth. There is only one place that you can discover the stability you need. Where? In God's Word.

All the answers we need are in the Bible. Everything we need to know to be fully equipped to live a truly victorious Christian life is in the Bible. Everything! Sometimes, the answers we're looking for can't be found — because we're looking for the wrong answers. We're looking for our answers instead of God's answers.

We must be doubly careful in searching for truth, in seeking solutions to our dilemmas. We must not be deceived by false prophets that teach a perverted truth, and we must be just as cautious concerning our own understanding of Scripture. We must learn to let the Bible speak to us, and stop speaking to it! We must listen for what God's Word is saying, not for what we want it to say!

How can you avoid being sidetracked from God's best by other voices? Get into the Word daily. Sit under the Word — in church — regularly. Become so immersed in Scripture, the whole Gospel, that you become totally familiar with God's voice. His Word is alive and powerful. Strength, discernment, and wisdom come from studying the Word. Bible study builds your faith. Faith comes by hearing, and hearing by the Word.

And this is where victorious living begins. I am a firm believer in victorious Christian living. It's a contradiction of terms for a Christian to be defeated! It's one thing to be saved and know you're going to heaven, and another to have abundant life right now. And feeling defeated isn't being defeated!

You've got victory, if you're a Christian, right now! I don't care what your circumstances are. It doesn't matter what kind of a situation you're in. You may be unemployed — but you've got victory! You may be separated from your spouse — but you've got victory. You may be desperately ill — but you've got victory! Your spouse may be unsaved — but you've got victory!

How do I know that you've got victory? Because the Word says so! Proverbs 24:10 states, "If you faint in the day of adversity, your strength is small." Just because you're a Christian doesn't mean you're exempt from problems. To say that getting saved lifts you out of the problems of the world onto a higher plane is wrong. That's not what being saved is all about. Being saved doesn't mean being "saved from problems," it means being "saved by grace." And that's better, anyway.

On our own, we would be overwhelmed by our problems. But, when we accept Jesus into our lives as Lord and Savior, we've still got to face problems, but we've got all the help we need! We can take our burdens to Jesus, and He'll give us the strength we don't have in the natural. He will give us the wisdom we don't have in the natural. He will give us supernatural resources.

When you can't love that scoundrel you live with anymore, Jesus pours the agape love of God through you. When you can't fight that disease in your body anymore, Jesus pours out His strength to revive you. When you can't find a job and your money is gone, Jesus provides a miracle to sustain you one more day. On your own, you are defeated. But in Him, you are victorious in the midst of problems.

Have you been enduring long? Days? Weeks? Months? Years? Is the devil dogging your steps, telling you to cash it in? Is he lying to you, telling you that you've been defeated? That God's not going to honor His promises? Who are you going to believe? The devil, or God's Word? What does God's Word say? What has God promised? He has promised to deliver us if we are faithful to Him, and that before the deliverance comes, He will be with us "through the valley of the shadow of death"! Tell the devil he's the liar — and you cling to the full truth of God's Word!

Let's take a look at some of God's promises. These are the ammunition you need to shoot the devil down when he comes gunning for your soul. The Word is your only true defense against him. And it's all you need.

He gives power to the weak, and to those who have no might He increases strength. Even the youths shall faint and be weary, and the young men shall utterly fall, but those who wait upon the Lord shall renew their strength; They shall mount up with wings like eagles, they shall run and not be weary, they shall walk and not faint (Isaiah 40:29-31).

When you feel weak, like you're going to spiritually faint, what do you need to do? Give up? No! You need to turn to the Lord. You need to wait upon Him and seek His face. He will renew your strength so you can press on in faith toward your deliverance.

In the New Testament, Paul states that in our weakness Christ is strong. It's just like the song the children sing that "we are weak, but He is strong."

Yes, the going gets rough sometimes and you feel so tired. Even Christ felt the pressures of spiritual weariness as He approached the time of His crucifixion. Yet, did He give up? Not at all. He turned to His Father in heaven, and His strength was renewed.

Have you ever heard someone say about another person, "Do you know what they're going through!" And they say it like an indictment, as if there's something wrong with the person going through the trial. They don't understand that it's better to be going through, than going down!

We all are faced with problems and troubles. Even me. But I'm going through them! I'm not going to get in the middle of the river and stop! I'm not going to get out in the middle of the flood and sink! I'm not going to drown in my sorrows; I'm going through them, with Christ leading the way.

Whatever the devil throws at me, with Christ I'm going through it. Whether it takes an hour, a day, a week, a year — in Christ I'll find the strength I need to endure until it's over.

Why? Because God has promised that His strength will sustain me, and when I've been faithful to Him in the trouble, He will give me the wings of an eagle to soar above it! Wow! What a victory! Just at the moment the devil thinks he's got you cornered, your spirit sprouts eagle's wings, and off you go!

> *But now, thus says the Lord, who created you, O Jacob, and He who formed you, O Israel: "Fear not, for I have redeemed you; I have called you by your name; you are Mine.*
>
> *When you pass through the waters, I will be with you; and through the rivers, they shall not overflow you. When you walk through the fire, you shall not be burned, nor shall the flame scorch you"* *(Isaiah 43:1-2).*

I want you to personalize this promise. Instead of reading "Jacob," insert your name there. And, put your name where it says "Israel." This promise is for you. God is telling you not to be afraid.

What's the first emotion that hits you when a crisis comes? Fear. And fear is a powerful emotion. It can emotionally cripple you, and affect you physically. Fear can cause you to "freeze up" or to become "paralyzed."

This often is why people who are afraid of the water drown. They may know how to swim, yet, when they fall into a deep lake, or into the sea, their fear overcomes them and they sink. Their minds are so gripped by their fear of the water that they can't even think to position themselves so they'll float. In fact, there are some people who are so irrationally afraid of water that they would drown even if it were only a few feet deep! They've allowed a fear to control a part of their life.

Fear is a great tool of the devil. There are some things we need to be afraid of, and that's why God's given us this emotion. Fearing the right things at the right times is beneficial, and can even save our lives. But the devil plays upon our fears, and perverts them.

The devil will take a simple fear, like the fear of animals, or the fear of high places, or the fear of people, and magnify it all out of proportion. And then, he'll shove your fear in your face and tell you you're no good. He'll hold that fear in front of you day and night until that's all you see. He'll take your eyes off Jesus and hold them on your fear.

Don't let it happen! When the devil says, "You're afraid!" you tell him, "But what do I have to fear? God's with me!" Get your eyes off your fear and on the Lord. Take your mind off your fear and get into the Word.

When you expose them to God's Word day in and day out, your fears will evaporate, just as darkness fades with the dawn.

A few years back I read a report in the newspaper about five people out West who survived a plane crash. They lived in a wilderness area for five days without food, water, or heat. After they were rescued, they were asked how they managed to survive. Do you know what kept them alive and safe? They said that each day, they gathered by the wreckage of the plane, and read God's Word. They were in the midst of a snowstorm, and they turned to God's Word! That's all they had, and it was all they needed.

I heard another story about a little girl stranded in a car in a snowstorm. She had her pet cat with her. Wanting to keep it warm so it wouldn't die, she placed the cat under her sweater, and bundled up in her coat. When she was found, the doctors stated that without the cat to help keep her warm, the little girl would have died. By taking only what she had and holding on to it, she survived.

What you have is enough! If all you've got is one Scripture to hang on to, it's enough. If all you have to give is one dollar, then it's enough. If all you have to cling to is your faith, then it's enough! God gives us what we need as we need it. I don't care what you're going through, or what the devil's been telling you, don't faint in your adversity. Look to God. He will give you strength and power to go on. He will give you the Holy Spirit's anointing. And it will be enough.

We have been named by God. He has promised His

presence even in the midst of fire and flood. We have
nothing to fear.

> *"Is not My word like a fire?"* says the Lord,
> *"And like a hammer that breaks the rock in pieces?"*
> *(Jeremiah 23:29).*

This is the strength of God's Word in our lives. It
will break the powers that bind us. It will destroy the
walls we've got our backs to. It will clear a way through
the mountain passes we must cross. Are you faced with
the persecution of a hard-hearted person? Apply the
Word of God to your life and the hardness will fade.
Do you feel cold inside because of bitterness? Apply the
Word of God to your life, and the coldness will turn to
warmth and love.

The devil never lets up. He is consistent in his attacks. We must be just as consistent in our application
of Scripture.

> *My son, fear the Lord and the king; do not asso-*
> *ciate with those given to change; for their calamity*
> *will rise suddenly . . . (Proverbs 24:21-22a).*

Are you in a good mood today? That's great, but I
don't like moody people! I hear a lot of Christians talk
about being in this mood or that mood. Today they're
in a bad mood because the weather is bad, and tomorrow they'll be in a good mood if the sun shines!

I'm happy. I'm not happy because I'm in a good
mood. I'm happy because I've got the joy of the Lord

in my life. It's in my life today. It was in my life yester-
day. And it will be in my life tomorrow.

Moods are not of the Lord. The Lord doesn't tell us
to "put on a good mood." He tells us to clothe ourselves
in His righteousness. We are to have the mind of Christ.
All day everyday. All year every year.

God doesn't want Christians who serve Him because
it feels good. He wants Christians who are committed
because it is good. We can't let our mood swings determine our walk with God. You can't live a victorious life
being a moody Christian. You must develop a consistency
in your spirituality. You must have one mind — a mind
renewed by God. James warns against being double-
minded. He says a person controlled by moods is
"unstable in all his ways" (James 1:8).

Victorious Christians are stable Christians. When
unexpected adversity comes along, they may be jarred
a bit, but they aren't knocked off center. The circumstance may stun them for a moment, but they re-
cover their senses quickly. It may look dark outside, but
they know the light will come in time.

Oh, it's easy to be happy when you win the lottery.
It's easy to feel secure when the bills are paid. It's easy
to be committed when there's food on the table and no
sickness in the house. When trouble comes, you may
not be happy about it, but you can still rejoice in the
fact that God is with you and the trouble will pass.

*Therefore take up the whole armor of God, that
you may be able to withstand in the evil day, and
having done all, to stand (Ephesians 6:13).*

Have you taken up your full armor, or just part of it? Have you done all you could, or just a little to get by? Many people who seem never to be victorious over trouble have given up too soon. They've covered one area of their life with God's armor, but left other areas open. They've gotten into His Word a little bit, every now and then. They don't feast on His Word every day. A big problem comes at them, they struggle a little while, throw up their hands and fall!

When is the devil going to hit you the hardest? At the beginning of your fast? At the beginning of your walk with Jesus when you're all excited? No, he's going to wait awhile and get you when your guard's down. Jesus fasted for forty days and nights before Satan showed up. And what's the first thing he said to Jesus? "Aren't you hungry? How about some fresh, warm bread?"

The devil didn't say, "I'll come back after you've had a big supper and a good night's rest." He hit Jesus at His weakest moment. And Jesus didn't respond with, "No, I shouldn't . . . but . . . well . . . if you insist!"

Jesus answered the devil with the Word of God. The devil came back at Him three times. Each time Jesus stood firm on the Word. Jesus didn't use one Scripture, and then quit. He used all the Scripture it took to send the devil on the run. Jesus did all that He could, and then stood firm on the authority of God's Word.

Victorious Christian living begins in the Word. Only as you become firmly rooted in the Bible will you be able to stand in times of trouble. But, standing firmly on His complete Word, victory is yours.

CHAPTER TWO

Armed for Victory

To be a victor — to live victoriously — means you have to have gone through a battle. And to go through a battle, you must be armed. As a Christian, you are involved in the most important battle of all — spiritual warfare. It's important that you understand what this means and what kinds of spiritual weapons are available to you. The victory is yours, but the battle must still be fought. You must be aware of the spiritual realm, understand what is happening there, and know your part in spiritual events.

Paul gives you a very clear glimpse into this world in 2 Corinthians 10:3-5:

> *For though we walk in the flesh, we do not war according to the flesh. For the weapons of our warfare are not carnal but mighty in God for pulling down strongholds, casting down arguments and*

*every high thing that exalts itself against the
knowledge of God, bringing every thought into cap-
tivity to the obedience of Christ.*

Further, in Ephesians 6:12, Paul again reminds you
that "we do not wrestle against flesh and blood, but
against principalities, against powers, against the rulers
of the darkness of this age, against spiritual hosts of
wickedness in the heavenly places." And something
very important to note is that Paul does not say some
of you are in the battle and some of you aren't. He states
that "we" are in the battle. All of us, whether you want
to be or not, whether you are aware of it or not, are involved in the spiritual warfare of this world.

What does this mean? Well, a very simple way to
look at it is that Satan is a spirit that you do battle with
daily. If you tried to deal with him strictly on a physical
level, you'd lose every time. If he were ever to
materialize in front of you and challenge you to a fist
fight — you'd be knocked cold if you took him on. But,
if you started "hitting" him with the Word of God —
dealing with him on a spiritual level — you'd overcome
him. While the devil can, through your spirit and mind,
afflict you physically, you cannot retaliate against him
physically.

But, you don't have to! Your spiritual weapons are
more powerful than any weapons any army on this earth
has ever conceived of. In Christ, you have more power
against Satan than is contained in an atomic bomb. Yet,
you must unleash God's power in your life.

Your first weapon is self-restraint, or, holding your

peace. Exodus 14:14 states, "The Lord will fight for you, and you shall hold your peace."

You must continually be aware that you aren't wrestling against flesh and blood. Your warfare isn't with people, but it is with the power behind the actions of people who do not know the Lord. Satan will come at you through others. Someone hurts you, or cheats you, or does you an injustice, and immediately you want to "get even." That's exactly what Satan wants you to do.

God doesn't want His children to retaliate against others. Scripture tells you to repay evil with kindness and love. This kind of action is like heaping hot coals on the head of your enemy! And kindness in the face of persecution is the best witness of Christ in you that you can offer.

The person that causes you problems is motivated by the evil in the world. At root, we're all motivated by good or evil. There is no neutrality in the spiritual realm. You must aim your anger at the evil behind the person, not at the person.

Plus, evil begets evil. Retaliation has a price. When you do evil to someone who has done you wrong, you stoop to his level, and you join the wrong side of the battle. When you "get even" the other person will lash back at you trying to "get even" and round and round you'll both go in a never-ending feud. Soon, instead of love and peace, your heart becomes infected and filled with bitterness and hatred.

When you hold your peace and let the Lord deal with the other person, amazing things can happen. First, the devil will be totally frustrated. He can't deal with love! Second, the person who is bothering you will either become your friend, or at least quit bothering you. And finally, others watching to see how you're going to react will respect you and be more open to letting you share the Gospel with them.

Your second weapon is the Bible, the Word of God. In the first chapter we looked at the power of God's Word. It's your best defense against the devil. But unless you get into the Word, and know it so you can use it, it's worthless. When you're on the front line of the battle, it's too late to discover you're out of ammunition!

Just having one hundred Bibles scattered around your house won't help you. The devil won't trip over the book, but he can be felled with the Word. You've got to read the Bible, learn the promises, and claim them in faith. You've got to load your gun before you can shoot!

There are twenty-seven thousand promises in the Bible. But they're useless if you don't know them and use them. When you apply God's Word in your life, the effect is powerful. You cannot get into the Word each day and come out negative and defeated. It's impossible. Victory is in the Word.

Jesus is the Word. The more time you spend in the Bible, the more like Jesus you will become. The more your spirit man is going to be changed into His likeness and image.

Kenneth Hagin tells a story that illustrates the incredible power of God's Word. At one of his rallies, he prefaced his sermon by saying, "I'm ready to preach the Word. I don't want anyone moving around, not even to go to the restroom. I don't want anyone to be distracted because the Word is powerful and it's going to change your life. If you are down, you're going to be up. If you're sick, you're going to be healed. Listen to the Word."

Then, he just began to quote the promises from the Bible. He literally was preaching just the Word. Suddenly he noticed a woman walking up and down in one of the side aisles. It bothered him, but he kept preaching.

He thought she'd sit down after a while, but she didn't. She just kept walking up and down in the aisle. Back and forth she went and it was bothering Brother Hagin to no end. Finally, he stopped his sermon, turned to the woman and said, "Madam, maybe you didn't hear me at the beginning. I asked everyone to please stay in their seats and listen quietly while I preached God's Word."

To his surprise, the woman came right down front, up on the platform, and walked over to him and took the microphone from his hand. "Brother Hagin," she said softly, "I'm sorry I'm disturbing you, but there's something you don't understand. When you started to preach, I was sitting in the back in a wheelchair. When you began to speak the Word of God, His power settled on me, healed me, and now I can walk!"

That's how powerful the Word of God is.

The third weapon you have is the name of Jesus. I wish just once the clouds of heaven would be rolled back so that you could see what really happens there when you call upon the name of Jesus. You do not fully realize the tremendous influence Jesus' name has in the spiritual realm.

John 14:13-14 states, "And whatever you ask in My [Jesus'] name, that I will do, that the Father may be glorified in the Son. If you ask anything in My name, I will do it." Over and over again in the New Testament, you see the phrase "in Jesus' name" used, and every time what was being asked for happened. Demons were cast out, dead people were raised to life, the sick and maimed were healed, and apostles were released from prisons.

I once heard about a situation where a person was praying for deliverance for a demon-possessed girl. This person prayed tirelessly for many hours yet there was no change in the girl. Finally, the person looked toward heaven and said, "Jesus, either there is power in Your name or there is not. I believe there is." And immediately the girl was released. Sometimes it takes persistence, but there is power in the name of Jesus.

There is a true story about a young couple who truly loved the Lord, yet the husband contracted a fatal illness. One night, as he lay upon his deathbed, his wife came into his hospital room to share his last moments. She knelt by the bed, and with tears streaming down her face, she breathed a prayer, "In the name of Jesus, don't let my husband die. God, give me back my husband."

When she looked up, her husband's body was lifeless. He'd died. Yet, something happened. The husband revived, and later told her what happened.

The husband, when he died, entered into heaven, and approached the throne of God rejoicing. Then, God pointed down to the earth, and the husband saw the hospital room where his dead body lay, and his wife crying beside the bed. God said, "You must go back! She's using that Name."

There is power in the name of Jesus.

The next weapon you have is your prayer language. Did you know that praying in the Spirit was a weapon? This is why the devil fights so hard against Holy Spirit baptism. He doesn't want you to pray in tongues! When you use your tongue to speak your prayer language, it becomes a sword that cuts the devil to ribbons!

So often, we misuse our tongues to speak evil against another. James warns against the sin of criticism, verbal abuse, and gossip. How much better to pray in tongues than to use your tongue to curse another.

When you find yourself in an argument, hold your peace, and pray to yourself in the Spirit. You'll be amazed at the peace that will flood your soul, and how quickly tension will disappear. When you are in a situation you don't understand and have no control over, pray in the Spirit. Romans 8:26 states, "Likewise the Spirit also helps in our weaknesses. For we do not know what we should pray for as we ought, but the Spirit Himself makes intercession for us with groanings which cannot be uttered."

Praying in the Spirit edifies your spirit. It builds you up and prepares you to stand in battle. It renews your mind. It plugs you in to the power of heaven.

I have been in a courtroom and watched as people

took the stand to lie, and Christians would begin praying silently in the Spirit, and stories would change in
the middle of sentences. I have watched people filled
with anger become subdued as those around them prayed
silently in the Spirit. Praying in the Spirit with your
prayer language will change the atmosphere around you.
It will break the power of Satan and charge the room
with God's presence.

Praying in the Spirit draws you toward the victory.

Another weapon, and one that is so often overlooked,
is fellowship. Have you ever heard people say that
they didn't need to go to church? They're full of baloney!
They are ignoring the injunction of Hebrews 10:23-25,
"Let us hold fast the confession of our hope without
wavering, for He who promised is faithful. And let us
consider one another in order to stir up love and good
works, not forsaking the assembling of ourselves together, as is the manner of some, but exhorting one
another, and so much the more as you see the Day
approaching."

The more you are around born-again, Spirit-filled,
dynamic, fruitful, beautiful Christians, the more you will
become dynamic, fruitful, and beautiful in your walk
with Christ. It is contagious. The worst thing you can
do when you're down and depressed is stay away from
church. You'll only get more depressed. You need the
fellowship of others.

The devil won't stay five seconds around one hundred Christians calling on the name of Jesus and praising God together. But, he will hang around one isolated
Christian who's a bit discouraged. What does the devil

tell you when you get discouraged, or when you make a mistake? "Stay away from church! Stay away from your brothers and sisters in the Lord!" He knows that if you get around Christians, you'll get supported, loved, and encouraged back to spiritual health.

Even Christ pointed out the importance and power of fellowshipping with others. In Matthew 18:19-20, He states, ". . . if two of you agree on earth concerning anything that they ask, it will be done for them by My Father in heaven. For where two or three are gathered together in My name, I am there in the midst of them." This is why the devil hates Christian marriages and is doing everything he can to destroy them. Some of the most powerful asserts of any church are the husbands and wives who are sold out to Christ and committed firmly to each other.

Psalm 22:3 states that God inhabits the praises of Israel, or His people. It doesn't say that He inhabits the praises of one person in Israel. He hears and desires your individual praise, and He answers your individual prayers. But He inhabits the praises of His people. God is with you always, but He is with you in infinite power when you are part of a believing fellowship.

As the timeless analogy teaches, it's easy to break a bundle of sticks one stick at a time. But it's more difficult, if not impossible, to break the bundle when the sticks are bound together.

What would have happened if after Jesus ascended into heaven the disciples had all scattered, each going his own way? Where would the Church be today? The devil loves division. He loves to scatter the flock and get each sheep isolated from the rest. If the devil can destroy Christian fellowship, he can destroy the Church of Christ!

But the disciples didn't scatter. Acts 1 describes what they did. They assembled together in one room and they "continued with one accord in prayer and supplication" (1:14). And as a result of their unity and fellowship, the Holy Spirit fell upon them, they spoke in tongues, and thousands of people were won to Christ in one day!

There is joy and strength in Christian fellowship.

Finally, your sixth weapon is praise. Psalms 148-150 tell you who and what should praise God, and when — everyone, everything, all the time! If you walk in praise, you will never walk in defeat. And the more you praise, the easier it gets. And the more powerful its effect.

Praise is a pleasing aroma to God, and a slap in the face to Satan. When you praise the Lord, the principalities and strongholds of the devil collapse. It totally confounds the intents of Satan when, after dumping a load of troubles on you, you stand and praise God. You aren't praising God for the troubles, but you're praising Him because He is with you and you have the victory.

Praise releases you from the power of problems. It lifts you up where eagles fly. When you begin to praise, you may not feel like praising, but as you do it anyway, joy begins to blossom in your heart. Peace that passes understanding begins to flood your mind.

How do you defeat a besetting sin? Every time you're tempted, praise the Lord instead. How do you keep from losing your temper? Praise the Lord instead. How do you overcome your fears? Praise the Lord! How do you revive your soul when you feel you can't go on? Praise the Lord!

Praise brings victory when all else fails.

CHAPTER THREE

Victory Begins in the Mind

Where does sin begin? In the mind. Before you commit a sin, you think about it. Every sin you commit is to some degree premeditated. At some point in time before you sin you've thought about sinning. It's through an undisciplined thought life that so many men and women get themselves into serious trouble.

In a very real way, what you think is what you are. What you put into your mind will determine what's in your heart, and what comes out of your mouth. If you don't put an evil thought in your mind, you won't have evil intentions in your heart. If you don't put wicked thoughts in your mind, you won't speak wicked words with your lips.

The mind is Satan's playground. All sin starts here. The longer you dwell upon a specific thought, the more power you give it. This works both ways.

This is why meditating upon the Word of God is so

effective. When your mind is filled with God's Word, there's no room for evil. When Scripture saturates your thoughts, His Word will sink into your heart, and His blessings will flow from your lips.

An imagination is a thought that's become more vivid. It's a thought with images and feelings added in. After a time, the imagination becomes a stronghold. It has your mind strongly in its hold, and you've yielded control of your thoughts to something else. Whether you yield to God or the devil is up to you.

Paul states in 1 Corinthians 2:16, "But we have the mind of Christ." Think about that for a minute. The implications are awesome. Satan knows the potential that you have if you start exercising the mind of Christ in your life. He'll do anything he can to distract you from holy thoughts. Satan will put all sorts of things in front of you to get your mind wandering away from the Lord. He understands the importance of the battle for your mind.

Are you using the mind of Christ that's in you? Or are you preoccupied with fears and doubts and worries? Some people get so overcome with worry they feel like they're losing their mind. Have you ever felt that way? It's a deception of the devil, for the Bible tells you "God has not given us a spirit of fear, but of power and of love and of a sound mind" (2 Timothy 1:7).

God has given you a sound mind. He has given you the power to overcome doubts. He has given you the ability to put away your fears. He has given you the mental strength to remain steadfast in Him.

All around you people are seeking peace of mind. But

they're looking in all the wrong places. They look for peace in sensuality, in the stock market, in drugs and alcohol. Instead of peace, they find dissatisfaction and emptiness. They ignore God, throw their lives into the clutch of Satan, and wonder why they're so tormented.

Some Christians have troubled minds. Why? Because they stay away from church most of the time. They avoid reading God's Word. They don't take time to talk with God in prayer. They sit in front of the TV all day watching game shows and soap operas. They let their eyes and minds wander over the things of the world. And they wonder why they're so troubled! They don't understand why they don't have peace of mind!

How do you have peace of mind? Isaiah 26:3 states very clearly that "[God] will keep him in perfect peace, whose mind is stayed on You [the Lord]." Is your mind troubled? What's in it? Kick out those things that are not of God, and start filling your mind with God's Word.

A pure heart and clean mind isn't automatic. It takes spiritual effort every day. The Bible says to take up your cross daily. You have to clothe yourself in Christ's righteousness daily just as you have to get dressed every morning when you get out of bed.

Ephesians 4:22-23 states, ". . . put off . . . the old man which grows corrupt according to the deceitful lusts, and be renewed in the spirit of your mind." And in Romans 12:2 you are told, "And do not be conformed to this world, but be transformed by the renewing of your mind, that you may prove what is that good and acceptable and perfect will of God." The key word in both Scriptures is renew.

Renewal is a process; it's not something that happens automatically when you are saved. Salvation opens your life to the Spirit, and begins the process of sanctification or renewal. And it's a cooperative process. Christ gives you everything you need to effect His renewal in your life, yet you must choose to implement His power. God won't force Himself on you. He created you with a will, the power of choice, and He wants you to choose to live for Him daily.

When you choose Him, He is right there beside you ready to hand you the tools you need for every situation you'll encounter during the day. If you don't ask for the tools, God will still be there, waiting patiently.

Everything you need to live a victorious life is available to you. "Now we have received, not the spirit of the world, but the Spirit who is from God, that we might know the things that have been freely given to us by God" (1 Corinthians 2:12).

The devil has two plans. His primary goal is to keep everyone he can from getting saved. He wants you and me in hell. But he also has a secondary goal aimed at those who become Christians. He wants to keep you defeated and down. And one way to do that is to keep you away from the Word and ignorant of God's promises. Hosea 4:6 says, "My people are destroyed for lack of knowledge."

Where do you find knowledge? In the Book of knowledge!

The devil will do everything he can to keep you away from the Word. He'll keep you busy, or make you sleepy, or give you a headache. He knows that if your mind becomes renewed through the power of the Word he's defeated!

Knowledge is essential, but you need the right kind of knowledge. Education is good and useful, but if your intellect isn't grounded in the Word, your learning is useless as far as your spiritual life is concerned. The devil often uses the tactic of trying to impress you and fill you with man's knowledge and make you think you "know it all." He'll let you read all the books about the Bible you want to read because he knows they won't renew your mind.

You need to read good Christian, Bible-based books. You need to read good Christian magazines and watch Christian TV. But, if you don't read the Word — get into it, and get it into you — all the Christian books, TV, magazines, and music won't renew your mind. Only God's Word can do it.

Satan will try to use your carnal mind, your unrenewed thinking, to trick you and confuse you. Often, you read the Bible and think, "Boy! That's just too fantastic to believe! I don't know if I can accept that." 1 Corinthians 2:14 warns that, ". . . the natural man does not receive the things of the Spirit of God, for they are foolishness to him; nor can he know them, because they are spiritually discerned."

God created you with the ability to reason. But, because of Adam's sin, under the Fall your reason is impaired. Therefore, your "natural man," or human reason often views the things of God as "foolishness," or unbelievable.

In your natural mind it is impossible to understand

and believe the things of God. That is why the world looks at you like you're crazy! As the verse says, spiritual things must be discerned with the spirit.

God's Word says that we are to have faith in Him — an "invisible" God! Satan engages your reason and tells you, "How stupid! Who can believe in someone that's invisible! If you can't see God, He's not there!" That's a reasonable assumption. But it's comparing apples with oranges, not "spiritual things with spiritual" as verse 13 says.

You are to discern God's presence with your spirit. You "know" God is there, not just because of the evidence of His creation, but because your spirit communes with His Spirit.

So many people lose their healing, or their miracle, or their faith because they've been reasoned out of them. Satan filled their minds with doubt saying they were foolish! Dumb! Stupid! And they listened to their minds instead of their spirits.

Romans 8:6 says, "For to be carnally minded is death, but to be spiritually minded is life and peace." If you let the garbage of negative, worldly thoughts clutter your mind, you will become spiritually dead. But if you "have the mind of Christ" in you, and learn to discern with your spirit, you will be filled with love and peace.

Do you want abundant life? Do you know where it's going to start? It's going to start in the way you think. You need to think big, spiritually. You need to think positive.

This goes far deeper than the world's formula for

positive thinking. It's more. It has to do with who and what you are in Christ.

It's more than bringing your carnal nature under subjection to the law of God. Romans 8:7 says, ". . . the carnal mind is enmity against God; for it is not subject to the law of God, nor indeed can be." Your carnal mind is always going to be alive and will always be your enemy. You're never going to get rid of it. You're never going to make it one of your friends. It will never be converted.

The only thing that's going to happen is that you can decide to quit feeding it, quit listening to it, and cast it down in the name of Jesus, and then let the mind of Christ have its place.

Philippians 2:5-6 states, "Let this mind be in you which was also in Christ Jesus, who, being in the form of God, did not consider it robbery to be equal with God." The biggest word in verse 5 is "let." The word let means to allow, or to give place to. You have to let the mind of Christ come into you.

Here is where your carnal mind will fight you. It will tell you there has to be more to it than this. There must be a struggle or a magic formula or something more. But that's not what the Bible says.

The Bible doesn't say "force this mind to be in you." It doesn't say "plead for this mind to be in you." It doesn't say "work to get this mind in you." The Word says to let this mind be in you.

What kind of mind? The same mind that Christ had. The mind that "did not consider it robbery to be equal with God." This doesn't mean that you and I are gods.

It means that you have in you the same Spirit that God has in Him. You are of God. God's image is in you. It means that when you let the mind of Christ reside in you, you will have the same faith Jesus had. You will think like Jesus did. You will see the way to victory with His eyes.

With the mind of Christ, you'll look at sickness and see the potential for healing. You'll look at a desperate situation and see hope. You'll look at a meager financial resource and see abundance. You'll look at an empty pantry and see a feast. You'll look at your troubles and problems and see victory.

CHAPTER FOUR

Victory Over the Flesh

One of the great teaching devices of Jesus was His use of the parable, or a story, to illustrate spiritual truths. Let's take a look at a very significant parable as related in Mark 4:

> *"Listen! Behold, a sower went out to sow. And it happened, as he sowed, that some seed fell by the wayside; and the birds of the air came and devoured it.*
>
> *"Some fell on stony ground, where it did not have much earth; and immediately it sprang up because it had no depth of earth. But when the sun was up it was scorched, and because it had no root it withered away.*
>
> *"And some seed fell among thorns; and the thorns grew up and choked it, and it yielded no crop.*

*"But other seed fell on good ground and yielded
a crop that sprang up, increased and produced: some
thirtyfold, some sixty, and some a hundred.*

*   *   *   *   *

*[And Jesus explained the parable to His disciples,
saying,] "The sower sows the word. And these are
the ones by the wayside where the word is sown.
When they hear, Satan comes immediately and
takes away the word that was sown in their hearts.*

*"These likewise are the ones sown on stony
ground who, when they hear the word, immediately
receive it with gladness; and they have no root in
themselves, and so endure only for a time. After-
ward, when tribulation or persecution arises for the
word's sake, immediately they stumble.*

*"Now these are the ones sown among thorns;
they are the ones who hear the word, and the cares
of this world, the deceitfulness of riches, and the
desires for other things entering in choke the word,
and it becomes unfruitful.*

*"But these are the ones sown on good ground,
those who hear the word, accept it, and bear fruit:
some thirtyfold, some sixty, and some a hundred"
(vss. 3-8, 14-20).*

I'm convinced that God's perfect will for His children
is that we produce a hundredfold — one hundred per-

cent — fruit in our lives. But there's a price to pay to achieve that goal.

Already, I've stated that the battle begins in your mind. But there are three dimensions to man. You have a body, a mind, and a spirit. And the battle takes place in all three areas. I believe the degree of your success as a Christian corresponds to how much of your life you've yielded to Christ.

The battle begins in the mind, but it doesn't end there. Many people fill their heads with a lot of facts about the Bible — theology and doctrine — yet go no further. They grasp the truth, but they've not incorporated the truth into their being.

Imagine you're hungry and you decide to have the leftover chicken leg in the refrigerator. You go to the kitchen and take the leg out and you stand there looking at it as you hold it in your hand. You know you're hungry. You know the chicken will take care of your hunger. You know it tastes good, and that it's nutritious. You know all about fried chicken legs. But until you take a bite of that leg, your hunger won't go away! Knowing about the chicken isn't enough. You've got to eat it — to incorporate it into yourself — before it's going to do you any good. And that's the way it is with God's Word and Christian living.

You take the Word of God into your mind, allow the Spirit to bring it alive within you, and then live it through your body in your behavior — what you do, what you say, who you are. A thirtyfold Christian has taken the Word into his mind, and stopped. A sixtyfold Christian has let it reach her spirit, and stopped; a hundredfold

Christian has let the Word permeate his or her entire being and life-style.

Romans 12:1-2 states, "I beseech you therefore, brethren, by the mercies of God, that you present your bodies a living sacrifice, holy, acceptable to God, which is your reasonable service. And do not be conformed to this world, but be transformed by the renewing of your mind, that you may prove what is that good and acceptable and perfect will of God."

To have God's perfect will in your life you must present your body as a living sacrifice. For many, this is tough. How is it done? Paul says simply, "Abhor what is evil. Cling to what is good" (Romans 12:9).

One thing I believe is greatly lacking in many Christians is maturity and growth. They lack the commitment to go on. So many become satisfied with the initial thrill of salvation, and try to maintain this experience. They cling to that initial zeal and excitement, nurturing themselves on milk and refusing meat. Soon, the milk is not enough and they fall out of the race. Some even repeatedly backslide and then go to the altar and get saved again and again. They suffer from spiritual bulimia.

Have you heard of this disease? Kathy Rigby, an Olympic gold medal winner, suffered from it. A person suffering from bulimia craves food all the time. They use food as a crutch for emotional problems. So they "binge," eating all manner of junk food and anything they can find. Yet, then, after a binge, they are consumed with guilt over having used the food as an emotional escape, and because they fear getting fat. So, they "purge" themselves by making themselves vomit. And the cycle repeats itself.

A person suffering from spiritual bulimia "binges" on backsliding, and when the guilt gets too high, goes to church to be "purged" by going to the altar, and getting saved all over again. And the cycle repeats itself.

Ephesians 4:22 states directly, "that you put off, concerning your former conduct, the old man which grows corrupt according to the deceitful lusts." Don't play with the world. Don't go back and dabble with old sins. Don't give the flesh an inch. Put off the old man, and "put on the new man which was created according to God, in true righteousness and holiness" (vs. 24).

Purge your mind of deceits. Purge your body of lusts. Purge your spirit of evil. And then feed daily — don't binge — on God's Word.

I believe the body is the final battleground for a Christian's life. You've given your mind to the Lord, and you commune with Him spirit to Spirit, yet, your body and its desires are still giving you problems.

Winning the battle for the body begins through an act of your will, and through the empowering of the Spirit. Here's the key. To have hundredfold success, all three areas of your being must be brought into submission to the will of God. Your success in one area often determines the degree of success in another.

To walk daily with God means presenting your body a living sacrifice to Him daily. You've got to choose to change old patterns, to defy old habits, to bring your life-style into line with His will.

It's just like coming to church on Sunday. You've got

to make a decision and quality commitment to doing it each week. When someone calls you to do something on Sunday, you've got to say "No! I'm going to church." When friends drop in on Sunday afternoon and want to spend the evening with you, you apologize and say, "I'm sorry, but I have church each Sunday night. Would you like to go with me?" When your body tells you it's too tired to get out of bed Sunday morning, or not feeling well enough to go out Sunday night, you tell it, "No! I'm going to church, body, and you're going with me!"

God wants your body in church. And He wants your mind in church. And He wants your spirit in church.

1 Corinthians 3:16 asks, "Do you not know that you are the temple of God and that the Spirit of God dwells in you?" Think about that a minute. Your body is a living church. A tabernacle where God comes to dwell. Your heart is a holy of holies. You are a walking, talking vessel for God's most Holy Spirit. And verse 17 warns, "If anyone defiles the temple of God, God will destroy him. For the temple of God is holy, which temple you are."

If you are not awed and moved by this verse, something's wrong with you. It's powerful and sobering.

We are God's living epistles. We are the Word of God made flesh, though not in the same sense as Christ.

God renews the mind, but the world cannot see our minds. God renews the spirit, but the world cannot see our spirits. How then can we reach the world with the Gospel? How can we draw our friends and neighbors into the Kingdom? How can we prove to disbelievers that God is alive?

By showing that God is alive in us. By presenting our bodies a living sacrifice, and thus being a living witness. By saying to those around us, "Listen to what I say, and watch also what I do. In me you will see God glorified."

Paul declares further in 1 Corinthians 6, "Foods for the stomach and the stomach for foods, but God will destroy both it and them. Now the body is not for sexual immorality but for the Lord, and the Lord for the body" (vs. 13).

Obesity, when caused from lack of willpower and good judgment, is a sin. To abuse food and overeat, thus literally deforming our bodies, is to defile the temple of God. There are a few people who have little or no control over their weight because of metabolism and other organic problems. Yet, they are very few.

Abusing the body with drugs is a sin. Or cigarettes. Or alcohol. Or coffee. Or pop. Or steak. Abusing any substance — even when it's normal food — is wrong.

Sexual immorality is wrong. Today, our world is literally plagued by the disease of sexual immorality of all kinds. Even many Christian leaders are allowing themselves to be infected through adultery, and even homosexuality. Just as there's a price to pay for God's glory, there's a greater price to pay for defiling His temple. The truth in this is readily evident as we read the headlines concerning AIDS, herpes, abortion, and teenage pregnancies.

Paul says in verse 18, "Flee sexual immorality." Take your body and run! Get your body away from sexual sin. Get your body out of the abortion clinic. Get

your body away from your seducing boyfriend. Present
your body a living sacrifice to Christ daily. Moment by
moment.

Paul concludes by reminding us again, "For you
were bought at a price; therefore glorify God in your
body and in your spirit, which are God's" (vs. 20). You
don't belong to the world. You don't belong to sin. You
belong to God. You don't belong to your boyfriend. You
don't belong to your adulterous lover. You belong to
God. You don't belong to the pusher. You don't belong
to your partying friends. You belong to God.

Victory over the flesh comes through getting your
priorities straight. It comes through deciding to serve
God each day, each minute, each second. On January
first, you can't make a resolution that "I'm going to
present my body a living sacrifice this year," and then
never think about it again. You'll fall before February
first!

Remember the parable about the sower and the seed?
What happened there? Some seed fell by the wayside,
some on stony ground, and some among thorns. The
first received the Word, yet immediately gave way to
Satan. They suffered from spiritual bulimia. The second
group received the Word, and were happy to receive
it, yet, they had no root. They did not become rooted
into the Word. It got into their minds, and no further.
When tribulation came, they were wiped out.

The third group took the Word into their minds and
into their spirits, but no further. When it came to presenting their bodies as living sacrifices, they couldn't
handle it. They wanted money. They wanted power.

They wanted sex. They wanted God in their hearts and minds, but they wanted their bodies in the world. What they didn't understand was that the world and its weeds will choke out the Spirit.

The final group Christ spoke about were "sown on good ground, those who hear the word, accept it, and bear fruit." How much fruit you bear depends upon how successful you are in allowing God to completely come into your life.

You must say, "I don't just want God's good will for my life. I won't settle for thirty percent living. I don't want God's acceptable will for my life, or just sixty percent victory. I want God's perfect will for my life. I want one hundred percent victory!"

This means when you hear God's still, small voice at night, without a moment's hesitation, you get out of bed, get down on your knees, and pray — instantly. Not only your mind and spirit, but your body responds to the call of God. Isn't that what you want?

If you want victory in your life, you must have victory over the flesh. And, in Christ, you can.

CHAPTER FIVE

Victory in the Desert

Are you going through a "wilderness" experience right now? We've all had them. The children of Israel had theirs, too. It lasted for forty years! Has any of yours lasted that long?

Most desert experiences are brief. But, the devil has a way of making mountains out of molehills. He's an expert at magnifying your problems way out of proportion.

God doesn't want that to happen. He wants you to keep your situation in perspective, and learn the lessons you need to learn. God knows what you're going through. He is aware of your problems. And He knows your limitations better than you do.

Recently, a pastor friend of mine and his wife were expecting their sixth child. Everyone was praying and believing that it would be a girl since the other five were all boys! Yet, of even greater concern was their financial situation. They needed a miracle.

The Lord laid it upon our hearts to be a blessing to them. We took up an offering, and took it to them personally. As soon as we handed them the love gift, the wife began crying. She was so upset and worried because they had no insurance to cover the baby's delivery.

The first thing that came to my mind was, "God knows that!" He'd just sent us to them with a love offering! God knew what their problems were, and He was already making provision for them. Yet, the wife was focusing on the problems instead of God's provision.

Have you ever done that? It's easy to do. We forget that God knows where we are. We cry out, "God, I'm out of work!" He knows that. "God, there's not enough money!" He knows that. When you're going through a desert place, it's easy to not hear God's voice, and to forget that He knows where you are.

We know the children of Israel often forgot that God was with them — and they even had the pillar of cloud by day and fire by night to remind them! Yet, even though they forgot about God, He didn't forget about them.

> *For the Lord your God has blessed you in all the work of your hand. He knows your trudging through this great wilderness. These forty years the Lord your God has been with you; you have lacked nothing (Deuteronomy 2:7).*

God reminded the children of Israel that He cared about them. Isn't it nice to be reminded that someone loves you? We all need that now and then. It's just like the husband and wife who were having serious problems and were considering a divorce. Finally, not wanting to divorce, they sat down to try and figure out what was wrong. Right away the wife said, "You've not told me you loved me for years!"

The husband was taken aback. "But, when we were married, I told you I loved you then. Nothing's changed!" "But," the wife replied, "I know you love me. But I still need to hear you say it."

Isn't that the truth for all of us? We like to be reminded that we're loved. And throughout God's Word, He gives us reminders of His love toward us. Even in the midst of a wilderness trial, we can be certain of God's care and concern and love.

But why do we go through these times? So that we can experience even greater blessing and growth. A lady attending our School of Ministry was out of work because of a strike at her plant. The strike was long, and extended over the winter. Yet, she came to services and testified, "My freezer has more food in it than when I was working! More of my bills are paid now than when I had a steady income!"

God's blessing is there for you, but there's a price for it. You've got to be obedient to His Word. You've got to walk in faith and holiness. You've got to bring your life into line with the Holy Spirit.

What happened with the children of Israel? Why did they even have to go into the wilderness? Because they doubted God's ability to provide for them. Why did they face so many hardships in the wilderness? Because they grumbled and complained against God. Even in the midst of His provision, with manna falling from heaven, they complained!

Have you ever done that? The real test of Christian living comes when times are good. It's when you have the money you need that you must spend it most carefully. You need God's guidance always — not just when times are tough. The price for daily blessing is daily obedience. You can't just name the blessings you want, claim them in faith, and live like the devil!

Romans 12:2 tells you the cost of Christian victory is "that you present your bodies a living sacrifice, holy, acceptable to God, which is your reasonable service." Either you serve God all the way, or you serve the devil. There is no in-between. God doesn't shower blessings on those who are lukewarm. He "spews them out" of His mouth.

Victory, or success in life, doesn't come from adopting the world's practices. It's not something God owes you, either. Any success or victory you achieve, you do so because of God's grace. And you don't come into God's grace through worldly success.

Dr. Ed Cole shared with me his experience. He said that he used to read a few Scriptures just before going to sleep each night, and he always kept his Bible on his nightstand. Yet, each morning at the breakfast table, he would read the Wall Street Journal. He read it faithfully, front to back. In fact, he carried it to his office with him and would continue to read it through the day.

Then the Lord started dealing with him. God revealed

to Dr. Cole that all the positive things he gained through reading a little bit of Scripture each night he was negating by filling his mind with all of the negative business and other bad news all day! What a revelation!

Christian victory, true spiritual success, begins in the Word. Not in the business magazines and papers. Not in the books on positive mental attitude. Not in the world's teachings on how to climb the corporate ladder. The only success worth having is found in the Word, and comes from living a dedicated, committed, faithful life, even when you're in the desert!

Trials make you better. And they prepare you to receive God's blessings more appreciatively. Going through a desert experience doesn't mean you are a failure. It means you either need to examine your life and renew your commitment to Christ, purging yourself of hidden sin, or, it means that you've been living in God's will and the devil's after you. But it doesn't mean you're a failure.

2 Corinthians 4:8-9 states, "We are hard pressed on every side, yet not crushed; we are perplexed, but not in despair; persecuted, but not forsaken; struck down, but not destroyed." Times are tough, but Christ in you is tougher. Life may deal you some hard knocks, but Christ is there to soften the blows.

Why do we suffer afflictions as Christians? Verses 16 and 17 explain, "Even though our outward man is perishing, yet the inward man is being renewed day by day. For our light affliction, which is but for a moment, is working for us a far more exceeding and eternal weight of glory."

Troubles don't come on Christians as punishment as much as they come for God's glory. God knows how much you can take, and He'll not allow you to suffer more than you are able. Yet, He will allow you to go through the desert from time to time because He wants to more fully reveal His glory to you.

Paul the Apostle knew what trouble was. He knew affliction. He was beaten, forced to run for his life, thrown in prison, and worse. Yet, in Romans 5:3-5, he proclaims:

> *And not only that, but we also glory in tribulations, knowing that tribulation produces perseverance; and perseverance, character; and character, hope. Now hope does not disappoint, because the love of God has been poured out in our hearts by the Holy Spirit who was given to us."*

James echoes this truth by stating, "count it all joy when you fall into various trials, knowing that the testing of your faith produces patience. But let patience have its perfect work, that you may be perfect and complete, lacking nothing" (James 1:2-4).

Easy living doesn't produce easy living! Easy living comes after living through the hard times. You may be laid off. You may be sick. And the devil is telling you you're a failure. That God is punishing you, or that He has forgotten you. Don't you believe it for a minute.

The bigger the need, the bigger the miracle God's going to give you. Don't let your faith shrink with your bank account. Don't starve your spirit when the pantry's empty. Don't put your heart in a sling when you get sick. These are exactly the things the devil wants you to do. God isn't punishing you because times are tough. But, if you respond the wrong way, you'll miss His blessing and be open to His judgment just as the children of Israel were.

Don't worry about the world's idea of success. That's not God's measure. You don't need a big house, a huge bank account, and a new car every year to be happy — or to be victorious! Everyone is called to a different life-style in the world, and Paul tells us to remain in the position in which we came to Christ (1 Corinthians 7:17-24).

Francis Schaeffer was a well-known Bible scholar and writer. He died in 1984 after battling cancer for years. In an interview, two years before his death, he was asked about how he dealt with his illness, and didn't it bother him that he wasn't healed by God. His response was simply, "Who am I to question the place where God has allowed me to come?"

How did Schaeffer live his life? Did he grumble and complain against God? Did he abandon his faith? No. He worked harder for the Kingdom than ever before. He knew the devil wanted him dead. He knew the forces of hell wanted to stop him from doing God's will. And He knew God cared about him and had his hand upon him. As a result, instead of being defeated, Schaefer's credibility was strengthened. Many more were open to listen as he preached and taught the Gospel if for no other reason than out of respect for Schaeffer's courage. He died from cancer, but he didn't die defeated!

So often, we want God's blessing right now. And we

want it all! When He gave the manna in the wilderness, God instructed the people to only collect enough for each day, and not to store any overnight, except for the Sabbath. He wanted to teach them the principle of His daily care. God will meet your needs each day just as you have need for that day.

The children of Israel didn't learn the lesson easily. Some tried to hoard the manna, and they paid the price for disobedience. They were greedy and ungrateful. Some of us are the same way. No matter how much we get, it's never enough. Someone gives you one hundred dollars, and instead of praising God for the one hundred dollars, you complain and say you needed two hundred dollars! God knows that. Did you need the two hundred dollars all at once? If one person gave you one hundred dollars, maybe another person was on the way to your door with the rest! You need to learn patience and trust from your trials.

God will give you victory in your desert. He is working in your life on your behalf. Don't have a pity party because all you can see is trouble. Open your eyes of faith. Activate the mind of Christ in you. Tell the demons the party's over and boot them out of your life! Stop complaining and moaning, and start praising the Lord. Call on the name of Jesus. Let God come down and tabernacle with you in the midst of your wilderness.

The devil will tell you that you're in a dry place, all alone. But you tell him he's a liar. God is with you. Then plant your palm tree of faith, spread the water of the Word at your feet, and bask in the presence of God's light as He places you in His oasis of love and care.

One of the greatest words you can use in time of troubles is "through." God didn't say that He'd take you into the river and into the fire. He said He's taking you through them! You'll go through the waters, but not be overcome. You'll go through the fire, but not be scorched. God will make a way for you to get through your desert.

Two young fellows in the church came to me one day and said they wanted to get their own apartment to share. But they didn't have the money for the deposit. However, they had checked with a bank, and could get a loan and wanted me to pray with them about it. They were a little unsure about taking out a loan for the deposit.

I'm not against loans. I believe God can use loans. But I believe there's a more excellent way. You can step into a higher realm, but there's a price.

As I prayed with the boys, I felt that God wanted them to wait. They agreed. Two weeks later one of them came up to me all excited. "Gary," he cried, "I tried to call you but you were gone on a trip! We had a miracle! Just a couple of days after we prayed," he explained, "my boss called me into the office. He said that for the last year the computer had miscalculated my pay checks. I'd been underpaid by $.18 an hour! The company caught the error and my boss handed me a check for the amount I'd been shorted. It was exactly enough for the deposit on the apartment, plus the first month's rent!"

If you believe God will meet your needs, even in the midst of your trials, He will. You can have victory in the desert if you trust in the Lord, live in obedience to His Word, and remain faithful in your daily walk.

CHAPTER SIX

Preparing for Victory

When God brought the children of Israel out of
Egypt, He made a covenant with them. The covenant
was an agreement that God made with them detailing
His promise to bring them into Canaan. After forty years
in the wilderness, God renews His covenant with them.
This is described in the book of Deuteronomy. They are
on the outskirts of Canaan, and Moses sits the people
down, and begins to review the last forty years.

Your Canaan is the blessing you need in your life.
If there's something God has promised to you, or
something you're believing for in His will, you can easily
compare your situation with that of the children of
Israel.

God told them that Canaan was theirs, but they had
to possess it. And to keep them encouraged as they
began to possess the land, God told them to recall the
past blessings and victories of the last forty years.

One of the first things they remembered was their release from Egypt and slavery. They were freed from bondage. You were freed from bondage to sin. Do you remember the day of your salvation?

The devil wants you to forget the things that God has done for you, and remember all the sins and mistakes from your past. Is there something ugly that happened to you? The devil will do everything he can to dig it up and throw it in your face. Recalling the past's failures will bring defeat.

We are not to recall our failures. We are to recall our victories over our failures. Do you remember when you were learning to ride a bicycle? How many times did you fall off before you managed to stay balanced? A lot, I'm sure. When you fell, did you stay down? You got up, right? You brushed yourself off and went on. God lifted you out of your sin and placed you on the rock of His salvation. Sure, you're a sinner. But you're a sinner saved by grace. Remind the devil of that, and keep pedalling in faith!

In Deuteronomy 6, the people are reminded of the commandments, and God says, "Write these words on your heart. Teach them to your children. Talk about them in your house and at work. Think about them when you go to bed and when you get up" (vss. 1-9). In fact, God tells the people to write the commandments on the doorposts of their homes and wear them on their foreheads!

Here's the pattern for family devotions. When your family is gathered around the dinner table, talk about the Lord. Read God's Word. Remind them of His commandments, and remind them of His blessings.

In Jewish homes, near the front entrance, there is a little bar-like fixture. It is called a mezuzah. Behind it, if you would unscrew it, you would find a hollow space containing a small scroll. Written on the scroll in Hebrew is Deuteronomy 6. They've written the promises on their doorposts.

I've been on a plane on the way to Israel, and several traditional Jews were on board as well. When it came time for them to pray, they stood up, put on their prayer shawls and phylacteries. A phylactery is a small black box containing the scrolls of Scripture. They placed them on their wrists and on their foreheads, just as they were instructed to do by God. They remembered God's past victories.

How, you wonder, could a people forget the great miracles of the Old Testament? How could the children of Israel forget God's blessings after forty years of seeing the pillar of fire each night and the pillar of cloud each day? Humans are fickle and forgetful. You don't have to read long in the Old Testament, especially in the prophetical books, to see how quickly the people forgot not only their victories, but the God who delivered them.

Are we any different today? The last time you found yourself in a financial crisis, what did you do? Did you sit and worry and fret and wonder how God was going to meet your need? Or did you recall the last time you needed money and the way God provided for you, and then praise Him for the answer He would bring this time?

God tells us to recall our past victories and be encouraged in our faith. Are you sick? Remember the last
time He healed you! Are you facing temptation?
Remember the last time He delivered you! Don't complain or murmur against God every time you stand up
and your back hurts. Thank the Lord for the last time
He touched you, and know that He will touch you again.

You need to write His promises and reminders of
past victories on the doorposts of your mind, and bind
them to your heart.

If we forget the victories of the past, the problems
of the present will seem bigger than they are.
Deuteronomy 7:17-18 says, "If you should say in your
heart, 'These nations are greater than I; how can I
dispossess them?' — you shall not be afraid of them, but
you shall remember well what the Lord your God did
to Pharaoh and to all Egypt."

This is what got the children of Israel into trouble
at the beginning of their wilderness experience. If they
had recalled the things God had just done for them, they
wouldn't have had to wait forty years to possess the
land. But, instead of recalling the victories, all they could
see was the problem of the present. Possessing Canaan
land seemed to them an impossible task. It was, without
God! But He was with them. He'd just brought them
out of Egypt and through the Red Sea. They watched
as the walls of water they'd passed between crashed in
upon the armies of Pharaoh!

Think of David as he encountered the situation with
Goliath. He has brought his brothers food and clothing,
and learns of the Philistine that is holding them at bay.

His soul is stirred and angered that the giant was mocking God and His people. He knew the giant could be slain. How? Because he remembered the past victories God had given him.

David went to King Saul and said, "I will go and fight this Philistine" (1 Samuel 17:32). What was Saul's reply? Did he say, Great! Go to it! I know you can do it. I've been looking for a hero. No, Saul told David, "You can't fight this Philistine. You're just a kid!"

Doesn't Satan have a way of using those around us to discourage us? Did you ever get some bad news, and the next thing you know you share your situation with another and they say, "Wow! That is bad!" You're looking for encouragement and they're just confirming the despair!

But, David didn't let Saul's reply get him down. He started recounting to Saul the various victories God had already given him. He told how he'd killed lions and bears when they would attack the sheep of his father's flock. He concluded by saying, "The Lord, who delivered me from the paw of the lion and from the paw of the bear, He will deliver me from the hand of this Philistine" (vs. 37).

Did David tell this to Saul to impress the King? No. He was recalling the past victories to encourage himself. He had already decided to face the Philistine, and through remembering the past, he was reinforcing his commitment to face the problem of the present. David did the same thing in the battlefield.

As he stood before the giant, Goliath cursed David and mocked him. It was pretty intimidating to see the monster up close, too. How did David handle it?

First, he told Goliath he wasn't there on his own. He had come in the name of "the Lord of hosts, the God of the armies of Israel" (vs. 45). Then, this time, he very matter-of-factly told the giant what he was going to do to him with God's help. He encouraged himself by stating the victory at hand. How could David be so confident? Because he had experienced God's deliverance before, and knew God would deliver him again. And He did.

Is there a "Goliath" problem confronting you right now? Remember the past victories God has given, and say to your "Goliath" as David said to his, "The battle is the Lord's and He will deliver me."

I really enjoy it when I'm invited to speak somewhere and I'm asked to share the testimony of what God has been doing in my life and ministry. As I'm speaking to the group, do you know who I'm really talking to? Me! Every time I come home from one of these meetings, I am pumped up and ready to go! There's no room for discouragement. There's no room for doubt. I've recalled the victories of the past and I know God will take care of me now.

Related to recalling past victories is having a vision for the future. This is what David was doing as he faced Goliath in the field. He had recalled his past victories, and based on those experiences, he stated his vision for the immediate future. David was saying, in effect, "God delivered me then, He'll deliver me now, and He's going to deliver me tomorrow."

Too many people are dwelling in the past. Too many people are focusing on their circumstances. You've got to set before you a vision of God's victory to get it.

I have seen dynamic things happen when people have gotten a vision of the power of intercessory prayer. Intercessory prayer gets your mind off your problems and on the things of God. It takes you out of yourself, and you learn compassion for another's plight.

You can sit around and moan and groan about your wife, your husband, your son, your daughter, or another loved one that's lost, and that's not going to save them. You can talk and gripe about your circumstances and the condition of the economy, and that's not going to help you. But when you start interceding, letting the Spirit of God pray through you, mountains are moved and glory comes down.

Writing to the Ephesians, Paul prayed that God would give them "wisdom and revelation" and that the "eyes of your understanding being enlightened; that you may know what is the hope of His calling, what are the riches of the glory of His inheritance" (Ephesians 1:17-18). He wanted them to catch a vision of God's glory. You need to take your eyes off your condition and look ahead to the end result.

You may not know the specifics of the outcome, but you know, based on the promises of God's Word, that whatever comes will be to God's glory and your benefit.

Standing at the entrance to their Promised Land, Moses sent out twelve spies to see what lay ahead. They returned with samples of the fruit of the land. It was truly a bountiful country God was giving them. Yet, forgetting the victories behind them, and ignoring the glory ahead of them, the children of Israel saw only the present circumstance. Giants roamed the land — the nations were strong and powerful! Surely the Israelites would be defeated!

When you stand on the threshold of your promised land, don't make the same mistake. God promises us victory, but we still have to work for it. We still have to possess it. Remember the victories of past trials you've come through, and look across to God's glory in the future, then go in and take the land.

The closer you get to possessing your promised land, the stronger the attacks are going to become. The devil's after you because you're not a mamsy-pansy Christian anymore, just warming a pew. You're on the offensive. You're moving in. You're going forward. And he's out to stop you any way he can.

I remember a story about a man who had gotten lost in the mountains in winter. The day had been sunny and mild, so he went out for a stroll on the paths near his cabin. As darkness began to fall, he looked around and realized he did not know where he was or how to get back to his cabin. He had no food, or even matches to start a fire for warmth.

He struggled along the path until it became totally dark, and he knew he had to stay put. If he walked further, he could walk right off the side of the mountain. So, he sat down just off the path, leaning against a large tree, and looked out across the dark valley.

Against the night sky he could see the outline of the next mountain. It was getting colder and colder, and he was having a hard time keeping warm. Suddenly, in the middle of the mountainside across the valley, he could make out a small campfire. He fixed his eyes on that fire and watched all night as it burned and glowed in the distance.

The next morning, shortly after daybreak, his friends who had been searching for him found him as he was walking along the path. They were happy, yet amazed that he survived. Their first question was, "How did you keep warm last night? It's a miracle you didn't freeze to death! We had record cold last night."

He smiled, and told them about the fire he had seen. He said that it had kept him warm. All night, he explained, he kept his eyes fixed on that distant campfire, and imagined he was sitting right beside it, basking in its warmth and comfort.

This man knew the warmth of past fires he'd sat by, and he caught a vision for the future. He took his eyes off his present circumstance and fixed them on his hope.

God told the children of Israel to get a vision of Canaan land before they went in so they'd have the strength and endurance to possess it. He took them up on a mountaintop and gave them a sneak preview of all that was to be theirs. And He told them to keep the vision before them, and they'd have the victory.

A woman once told me that she had been overweight and struggling to slim down. One day she sensed God directing her to buy a new dress — the size she wanted to be. So she did. She went out and bought a dress two or three sizes smaller than what she wore. It was a beautiful dress, too. She hung it up on the back of her closet door where she saw it every day.

And each day as she got dressed, the devil would make fun of her. He would tell her she was silly, that she'd never fit into that tiny dress. And she would respond back, "I'm going to fit into that dress for the glory of God!" She had a vision of where she wanted to be. She was walking with God in faith. And she's wearing the dress today!

Even preachers need to have a vision of what God can accomplish. A friend of mine used to give altar calls after every service, yet no one ever came forward to accept Christ. God dealt with him, and asked him if he was really expecting anybody to get saved. He wasn't!

After that, he said that before giving an altar call, he'd close his eyes and see people running to the altar. Nothing happened at first but he kept his vision in front of him. He began to expect people to come forward. He anticipated them coming forward.

One night, the vision took hold. Before he even preached, he sensed the victory at hand. He said the most powerful anointing fell upon his preaching, and when he gave the altar call, people ran to the altar. They came one at a time. Two at a time. Five at a time. A dozen at a time! And they kept coming. Revival swept that church because the pastor caught a vision of God's glory and held on by faith.

Fred Price relates the story of how it was when he first started his present church. The church had long pews then, instead of individual seats. He said the service would start, and fifteen minutes later half the people would come in, then ten minutes later more would trickle in, and so on. Then, as they would settle down, they'd take off their coats, lay them down in the pew and take up three or four spaces.

One day he told his people, "You mark my words. The day's coming when you're going to stand in line to get into this church." He had a vision of people filling the church, of people coming early to get a good seat. And it began to happen. And they come early or stand in line today to get into that church.

The final step in prepartion for accepting God's victory is to understand why you are to live in victory. Why did God give you past victories? Why do you need to have a vision of your future hope? Because it is a fulfillment of God's purpose for your life.

Deuteronomy 7:6 states, "For you are a holy people to the Lord your God; the Lord your God has chosen you to be a people for Himself, a special treasure above all the peoples on the face of the earth." You are special to God and He has a special purpose for you.

Did you know that you were created for His pleasure? That you were made to accomplish positive things and that even before you were saved, God had a special job for you to do? He was just waiting for you to accept Him so He could appoint you to your purpose. Ephesians 2:10 declares, "For we are His workmanship, created in Christ Jesus for good works, which God prepared beforehand that we should walk in them."

As sinners we are outside of God's will and purpose. We are going our own ways, following a path that leads to destruction. Yet God didn't create us to go to hell. He wants us to be all we can be in His army! And, even while we were yet sinners, He loved us, and had a plan and purpose prepared for us that, if we chose it, would lead us to glory and heaven.

It's all a matter of choice. When we choose to accept
Christ, we must still choose to walk in His Spirit every
day. Whether you walk according to God's purpose or
the devil's is your decision.

Let's imagine that someone died and left you a mansion. Just because it's now yours, are you automatically
living in it? No. You have to move. Before you move,
you've got to decide to move. Remember, victory begins
in the mind.

What if you say, "It's a beautiful mansion, and I'd
really like to live there, but moving's so hard!" Who's
to blame for your not possessing the mansion, you or
the person who left it to you?

There are people who've complained and grumbled
for years against God, saying His promises are false.
That God's a liar. Yet, they've never taken the first step
of committed, persevering faith. They've not made a
move toward possessing their promised land.

You've got to choose to step into the purpose God
has prepared for you to see it fulfilled. And you need
to renew your choice daily.

God has chosen you to possess the land. He's sus-
tained you in the past, even while you were yet unsaved.
And, He promises the hope of glory and heaven. Do you
want victory in your life? God does. He's shown you victory before, and He's ready to give you victory again.

CHAPTER SEVEN

Turning Troubles
Into Triumphs

The story of Joseph is an amazing one. It begins in Genesis 37. Joseph was seventeen and worked as a shepherd tending his father's flocks. His father was Jacob, renamed by God, Israel. Joseph was truly a favorite son, and Jacob expressed his love by giving Joseph an exquisite new tunic of many colors.

At this, Joseph's brothers became very jealous, and verse 4 states, "they hated him and could not speak peaceably to him."

When you became a Christian, how did your unsaved friends react? Were they delighted, or irritated? This is the kind of situation Joseph's story illustrates. Plus, it gives us a perfect example of how to properly respond to adversity, and turn our problems into victories.

Then, Joseph had a dream. He dreamed that he and his brothers were in the field binding sheaves. Suddenly Joseph's sheaf stood up, and his brothers' sheaves bowed down before it. Joseph had a second dream, and in it, "the sun, the moon, and the eleven stars bowed down" to Joseph (vs. 9).

How did his brothers react to these dreams? "They hated him even more" (vs. 5). And in verse 11 it says his brothers "envied him."

When we become Christians, our worldly friends often turn against us. And what's worse, sometimes, as the Lord begins to bless us and use us in ministry, even our Christian brothers and sisters may begin to envy us. Has this ever happened to you?

Yet, Joseph's situation became more serious than yours or mine is likely to become. Later, as he and his brothers watch the flocks, the brothers conspire against Joseph, and sell him into slavery. They take his tunic, tear it and sprinkle it with goat's blood, and tell Jacob that Joseph has been devoured by a wild beast (vss. 12-36).

If anyone had a reason to complain and grumble it was Joseph. Imagine his despair. He was beaten by his brothers, sold into slavery, and separated from his father whom he loved dearly. What would you have done in that situation? A lot of us would have cried out to God, "This isn't fair! Why are You doing this to me, God? I'm not going to take this! What's the use of being a Christian?" And we would have abandoned our faith.

That's not what Joseph did. The next mention of him is in Genesis, chapter 39.

The Lord was with Joseph, and he was a successful man; and he was in the house of his master the Egyptian. And his master saw that the Lord was with him and that the Lord made all he did to prosper in his hand. So Joseph found favor in his sight, and served him. Then he made him overseer of his house, and all that he had he put under his authority.

So it was, from the time that he had made him overseer of his house and all that he had, that the Lord blessed the Egyptian's house for Joseph's sake; and the blessing of the Lord was on all that he had in the house and in the field. Thus he left all that he had in Joseph's hand, and he did not know what he had except for the bread which he ate. Now Joseph was handsome in form and appearance (vss. 2-6).

Sounds like Joseph had it made, right? He remained faithful to the Lord and the Lord prospered him, even in slavery. But what happens when you're doing what God wants you to do? Does the devil leave you alone? He didn't leave Joseph alone either.

In verse 7, we're told how his master's wife tried to seduce Joseph. He refused. She insisted, and took hold of his garment. Joseph turned and ran out of the house. Yet, the woman had such a strong grip on his robe that she pulled it off him as he fled.

That evening, angered and embarrassed that Joseph would refuse her charms, she took his tunic before the master and concocted a story claiming that Joseph tried to rape her. Immediately, without opportunity to defend himself, Joseph was thrown into prison.

It wasn't bad enough that he'd been beaten, separated

from his family, and sold into slavery in a foreign land.
Now he was in a stinking prison for a crime he did not
commit! I'm sure that most of us, if we'd made it that
far, would drop out at this point. Joseph had been
faithful to the Lord. Did he deserve this? No. But neither
do we deserve God's mercy! Sometimes, getting what
we deserve isn't what we need. Getting God's best is
more important.

Even in prison, Joseph was faithful to the Lord and
his godly walk. Verse 21 states, "But the Lord was with
Joseph and showed him mercy, and He gave him favor
in the sight of the keeper of the prison." Joseph was
put in charge of other prisoners and was made responsible for their care. And he did his job well, without complaining or rebuking God.

> *The keeper of the prison did not look into
> anything that was under Joseph's authority, because
> the Lord was with him; and whatever he did, the
> Lord made it prosper (vs. 23).*

Look closely at this verse, and at verse 2. Notice the
phrases "he was a successful man," and "whatever he
did, the Lord made it prosper." We hear a lot of teaching
today about prosperity and success. We hear it from
Christian teachers and read about it in Christian publica-
tions. And these themes are just as popular in secular
situations. Everyone wants success and prosperity.

But no one is thinking in terms of the kind of success and prosperity Joseph experienced. In fact, by our
standards, we'd consider Joseph a dismal failure. He

couldn't do anything right. He couldn't keep his mouth shut and stay out of trouble with his brothers. He couldn't even manage to handle his master's wife. He was a two-time loser. First slavery, and then prison.

Yet, the Word declares that Joseph was successful and prosperous, and that the Lord was with him, and showed him mercy. A lot of people want success, but they don't want it on God's terms. They want it on their own terms.

Success in life for many is to have all the money they want, not just what they need. It means getting the clothes and house and car they want, not just what they need. It means being free from every trouble all the time. And this isn't God's idea of success.

Many who seek success outside of God's guidelines find that instead of freedom, they become slaves to things and appearances. Instead of prosperity they find emptiness in their souls. God wants us to be successful in Him. He wants us to be prosperous in His Spirit. He wants to give us peace and liberty in the midst of problems and troubles.

Success as a Christian comes through obedience. It comes through faithfulness. It comes by passing through the fire and through the water. It doesn't come on a silver platter with no effort and no cost. If you want spiritual success, you must pay the price of perseverance. You must meet the cost of commitment.

Joseph's ordeal didn't end in the prison. God doesn't leave us in the wilderness. Joseph became known as an interpreter of dreams, and Pharaoh had a dream that needed an interpretation. All of Pharaoh's wisest leaders were of no use to him. But Joseph gave him the answer. Almost overnight, Joseph ascended through the ranks of Egyptian government into a place of prominence and power.

In fact, as a result of a famine, he was put into a position where he could do anything he wanted to his brothers. If he had wanted, he could have finally gotten even.

Isn't that what you and I would have been tempted to do? After having been a slave and a prisoner, cut off from our parents and friends for years, we'd be a little angry at those responsible. But retaliation, as we've learned, is never right. It always backfires. If we are truly Christians, our response to our enemies and persecutors will always be a response of love and forgiveness.

Joseph was truly a godly man. After carefully controlling the situation to be assured that his family was safe and to get his father into Egypt, Joseph dealt with his brothers after the death of their father.

In chapter 50, verse 15, his brothers consider their fate: "When Joseph's brothers saw that their father was dead, they said, 'Perhaps Joseph will hate us, and may actually repay us for all the evil which we did to him.' " If anyone had a reason to hate these scoundrels, it was Joseph. He had very real, substantial reasons to want to get even with them. But having a reason to get even never gives us the right. As Christians, our responsibility to love one another always cancels our rights for doing harm.

Finally, Joseph faced his brothers, and took the final

grand step in turning his troubles into ultimate triumph. "Joseph said to them, 'Do not be afraid, for am I in the place of God? But as for you, you meant evil against me; but God meant it for good, in order to bring it about as it is this day, to save many people alive. Now therefore, do not be afraid; I will provide for you and your little ones.' And he comforted them and spoke kindly to them" (vss. 19-21).

The devil went crazy! And you can make the devil go crazy, too. That verse, Genesis 50:20, has become a key in my life. God took what the devil intended for harm and turned it around for good. He's done it for me over and over.

So often people face trials and throw the blame on God! They end up sick, and say, "God, You put me here!" Their business falls apart, and they cry, "God, why me?" Families begin to disintegrate and someone says, "What did I do to deserve this, God?" And virtually every time, the attack was from the enemy and God was standing by ready to help. But instead of seeking His help, we've lashed at Him in anger.

I've said it before and I'll say it again. God doesn't promise easy street when we become Christians. He promised us that whether our paths were easy or hard, He would always be at our side.

In 2 Timothy 3, there are some powerful promises, and some surprising ones. Verse 12 states, "Yes, and all who desire to live godly in Christ Jesus will suffer persecution." Can you say amen to that?

There are two teachings currently popular that are wrong. One, I've mentioned already, says that Christians aren't supposed to have problems. And the second one says that if you are having problems, it's always because of sin in your life. This isn't what the Bible teaches.

When things go wrong, it's good to examine our lives and make sure everything is in order. It is possible that there is some hidden sin that we need to get rid of. Yet, that's only one reason we have problems. Sin causes problems. Satan causes sins and problems!

The Psalmist stated that many are the afflictions of the righteous. The Bible is full of declarations that believers are going to have tough times in this world. Paul says that all creation is groaning to be released. And we will be.

Hebrews 11:24-26 reveals the character of Moses:

By faith Moses, when he became of age, refused to be called the son of Pharaoh's daughter, choosing rather to suffer affliction with the people of God than to enjoy the passing pleasures of sin, esteeming the reproach of Christ greater riches than the treasures in Egypt; for he looked to the reward.

How many of us are just the opposite? We disdain the reproach of Christ, and go after the passing pleasures of sin. Instead of denying the world, we embrace the world. Many try to live with a foot in both the world and the Kingdom. It can't be done. God won't accept compromise.

Some of you spouses, if you would only give in to your mate and deny your faith, things would go a little easier at home. But as it is, your home is hell because of your commitment to Christ. Some of you face ridicule at work because you refuse to be "one of the guys" and cuss and chew and tell dirty stories.

Some have started tithing faithfully on what little income they've got, and have been hit with a big financial burden. You're suffering because you've chosen to serve and sell out to God. You're being hit with affliction because you're after a greater prize than earthly success.

Instead of cursing God when trouble comes at you, curse the devil! Tell him God's on your side working his evil for greater glory. Remember Joseph and his perseverance and faithfulness. Are you suffering as much as he did?

In Hebrews 12:1-4, Paul describes the Christian walk as a race. It takes endurance, but God is before us. And finally, he describes the hostility and shame Christ experienced, and says, "You have not yet resisted to bloodshed, striving against sin" (vs. 4). Did you know that many of the apostles and early Christians were brutally tortured and killed for their faith? Some were sawn in two. Some were beaten and hanged. Others were thrown to lions for sport.

Is your boss whipping you? Are there any lions in your house? Have your friends come over with their saws in hand? So, what have you got to complain about? Look to Christ, the author and finisher of your faith, and, like Joseph, let God turn your trial into triumph.

Deuteronomy 4:30-31 instructs you, "When you are in distress, and all these things come upon you in the latter days, when you turn to the Lord your God and

obey His voice . . . He will not forsake you. . . ." The
first thing to do in tribulation is run to the Lord, not
away from Him. You must call out to Him, not throw
curses at Him.

God is on your side. He wants you to have victory.

There are those who get into a crisis in the middle
of the week, and stay away from church on Sunday. You
go and ask them why they weren't in church, and they'll
start in telling a big sob story of how bad their week
was, and they were so discouraged, and blah, blah, blah.
Baloney! They should have run to church and gotten
there early. They should have said, "Open up! I can't
wait to get in! I need to hear God's Word. I need the
fellowship of the saints! The devil's come against me
and I need strength to beat him off!"

Don't run from God. Don't run from church. Don't
avoid your brethren in the Lord. This is just what Satan
wants you to do. Turn to God and He will deliver you.
Turn to the church and you will be encouraged. Turn
to your brothers and sisters and you will be lifted up.

Want to really set the devil on his ear? When he
shows up, smile. When he dumps troubles, laugh in his
face. John 16:33 admonishes, "In the world you will
have tribulations; but be of good cheer, I have overcome
the world." That should set your feet to dancing!

Jesus says be happy when you're troubled! Rejoice!
Relax! He is in control. James 1:2 says, "Count it all
joy when you fall into various trials." Why? Because
trials produce a strong Christian character.

The devil means to do you harm when he sets temp-
tations and trials in your path. But God turns the trouble

into triumph when you remain faithful, and He builds you up stronger than before.

A local businessman had trouble with neighborhood boys throwing bricks through his store window, and breaking in. So, the man had the old glass replaced with thick, tempered glass. The boys came back and threw their bricks. The glass shattered, but didn't break, just like a windshield on a car. The boys couldn't get in. The man learned from his trial that he had a weak spot in his store, so he made it stronger.

Tribulations produce Christian character and spiritual strength. When things get tough, you need to turn to the Word, stay close to God, count it all joy, and continue in the faith.

Praise God in the midst of your trials and it can change the whole situation. Remember Paul and Silas when they were in prison? Did they grumble and complain? No. If they had, they'd still be in prison! Instead, they began to sing praises unto the Lord. God responded, shook the foundations of the prison, and the doors were opened.

A minister friend of mine was coming up to Pittsburgh to hold a meeting. He was running a little late when he had a flat tire and had to pull off the road. He discovered he didn't have a spare, and began to get discouraged. He said, "God, I'm on my way to a meeting to preach Your Word, and now look!"

As he stood there feeling a bit glum, the Lord impressed upon him that he should dance around his car and begin praising God. Right there on the turnpike! Somewhat reluctantly, he closed his eyes and started to praise God as he moved around his car.

He only got around it one time when a big semi pulled over behind him. It was the kind of truck they haul new cars with, and it was empty. The trucker offered to put the minister's car on his rig and drive him to the next service station. He got his car fixed and made it to the meeting on time.

You need to glory in your tribulation because God will turn it around for your glory! And Christ will be glorified in you.

> *Beloved, do not think it strange concerning the fiery trial which is to try you, as though some strange thing happened to you; but rejoice to the extent that you partake of Christ's sufferings, that when His glory is revealed, you may also be glad with exceeding joy. If you are reproached for the name of Christ, blessed are you, for the Spirit of glory and of God rests upon you. On their part He is blasphemed, but on your part He is glorified . . . Yet if anyone suffers as a Christian, let him not be ashamed, but let him glorify God in this matter (1 Peter 4:12-16).*

Every time the devil does something to you or against you because you're a Christian, God says I'll pour my spirit of glory out upon you in a greater way. So, what the enemy sent for evil to get you down, God can use to make you a stronger person. You can turn your trials into triumphs if you react Scripturally.

Don't get down or let it blow you away. Don't get

overcome with discouragement. Continue steadfastly in the Word and give glory and praise to God.

God will bless you now, bringing you through your trials, and you will have a great reward waiting for you in heaven. The next time something goes wrong, shout and leap for joy, and turn your troubles around!

CHAPTER EIGHT

Ingredients for Victory

If you've ever baked something or prepared food from a recipe, you understand the combination of various ingredients. Every recipe consists of individual ingredients. For baking, you need flour, eggs, salt, milk, water, and so on. Each ingredient by itself is useless to produce the cake, pie, or cookies you want.

What would happen if you took an entire bag of flour, dumped it into your cake pans, and put them in the oven? Would you get a cake? No. You'd have a mess of hot flour! And it wouldn't be very tasty, either. Sugar by itself is sweet, and it tastes good in small quantities. But would you like to eat sugar cookies that were all sugar and nothing else? How do you think your family would respond if you gave them sugar "sugar" cookies to eat, and a bottle of vanilla to drink? Yuck!

You need flour and sugar and vanilla and other ingredients to bake sugar cookies with. But the ingredients must be mixed together, and blended. You can't make cookies with only one ingredient. You need them all.

The same is true for victorious Christian living. You need the supernatural and the natural, blended together. One part natural, and one part supernatural.

The book of Exodus tells the story of how the children of Israel were delivered out of Egypt through Moses. Do you remember how Moses was called to leadership, and how he responded? He was tending the flock of his father-in-law, and suddenly he spotted a bush burning.

What was so unusual was that the bush burned, but did not burn up! The bush remained whole within the flame. Naturally, this got Moses' attention, and he went to investigate. And then God spoke to Moses.

God laid out the whole story to Moses and Moses didn't say a word. God explained that He had heard the cry of His people, and they would be delivered. Who would be their leader out of bondage? Moses, of course!

Now Moses spoke. "Who, me?" Can you identify with Moses? Have you ever seen a need that no one was ministering to, and you prayed that God would raise someone up, and He told you to meet that need? That wasn't what you had in mind, right? We're always ready for someone else to heed the call, but we're seldom ready when the call names us!

God responded to Moses, "Yes, you! And, of course, I will be with you."

Certainly, that's enough reassurance for Moses, right? No. He began to do exactly what you and I tend to do when God calls us to service. We start listing our inadequacies, our shortcomings, our faults. We do our best to convince God we're not worthy, that He's made the wrong choice.

What we don't understand, and what Moses failed to understand, is that when our natural abilities are tied to God's supernatural resource, we become more than adequate for the task.

When God calls us, we must keep in mind two things. First, God doesn't make mistakes. He doesn't choose the wrong person. He knows exactly who is right for the job, and who He wants for the job. If God is God, and He chooses you, who are you to argue with God? Think about that a minute.

Second, God knows you better than you know yourself. He knows all of your inadequacies. He knows about shortcomings you're not even aware of! He doesn't need you to read Him a list of all your faults and weaknesses. He made you.

When God chooses you or me for a job there is no excuse we can't serve Him. None. There are no reasons we can give God to get us off the hook. Zero. When He tags you, you're it, ready or not. And if you weren't ready, he wouldn't tag you. God knows exactly what He's doing even if you don't. We're called to trust God, not argue with Him.

Moses knew better, but still he started running through his big list of big weaknesses. And he listed some very common excuses that we use today. Look at chapters 3 and 4. "I'm a nobody," said Moses. "No one's going to pay any attention to me. I don't have clout. I'm not a good speaker. I don't have enough authority. I've not been trained for this. I've not been to seminary yet. I'm just a sheep herder. Joe's got a better education; use him. How can I prove You called me? Linda's got more talent than I do; use her." And so it goes.

In fact, God chose Moses for a task that would require him to develop his weakest trait — speaking in public. In Exodus 4:10, Moses pleads, "O my Lord, I am not eloquent, neither before nor since You have spoken to Your servant; but I am slow of speech and slow of tongue."

What's he saying? He stutters. He can't think on his feet. He gets tongue-tied. His knees knock when he's called on to pray in public. And this is the way he's ALWAYS been.

How many of us have told God things like this? "But, God," we cry, "there's no way I can be a preacher! I've ALWAYS been terrified of groups!" Or, "God, I've ALWAYS been shy! I can't sing a solo!" Or, "But God, I've ALWAYS tripped over my own feet. I can't be an usher!"

We need to understand who God is, and who we are in Him. In verse 11, God reminds Moses Who is in charge of whom: "So the Lord said to him, 'Who has made man's mouth? Or who makes the mute, the deaf, the seeing, or the blind? Have not I, the Lord?' "

Who made you? Who made you the way you are? Who has given you the talents you have? Who has given you the skills, abilities, and personality that make you so unique and special? The one and only true God, your Creator and your Lord.

When God calls us, we need to remember that God will take the natural ability which He has given us, and blend it with His supernatural resource. On our own, we're right about being failures. We need God to minister successfully. And when He calls us, He adds the missing ingredient we need. He takes our natural abilities (which He gave us) and mixes them with His supernatural resource.

Finally, Moses gets the picture. Although God had to get Aaron to help him, Moses went to plead his case before Pharaoh to release the children of Israel from slavery.

This is going to be easy, right? After all, God called Moses for this specific purpose. God's behind him all the way, so there are no obstacles to overcome, right? Wrong. Moses was in God's perfect will, but he still faced opposition and trial. Remember how we discovered that we're not doing battle in the fleshly realm, but in the spiritual? We need to keep this in mind. What may seem easy to our fleshly eyes isn't so easy when we look at it from a spiritual perspective.

Moses stood before Pharaoh and told him God commanded that he let the people go. Pharaoh responded, "Who is the Lord, that I should obey His voice?" And then he doubled the Israelites' workload.

Moses wasn't merely going up against flesh and blood. There was a far greater power at work. The power of hell was behind Pharaoh's answer. The battle was going to get spiritually violent.

Each time Moses made a move, Pharaoh made a counter move that increased the misery of the Israelites.

Isn't this so typical of the Enemy? You're on the threshold of deliverance and victory, and Satan pours on the trouble even harder than before. Why? He knows he's about to be wiped out, and he's after all the casualties he can take down with him.

What does God do with trouble? Moses didn't know what was going on. He went to God and began to ask questions. "So Moses returned to the Lord and said, 'Lord, why have You brought trouble on this people? Why is it You have sent me? For since I came to Pharaoh to speak in Your name, he has done evil to this people; neither have You delivered Your people at all.''

Moses made a common mistake. Moses assumed that because God had called Him he could take his rod, wave it like a magic wand in front of Pharaoh, and say, "Abracadabra, let my people go." Then with a flash of fire and a puff of smoke, out of Egypt they'd march. That's not the way God said it would be, nor is it the way He works.

A lot of Christians try to use their faith, or even the name of Jesus, like a magic wand. They take their checkbook in their hands, bow their heads, and say, "In the name of Jesus, checking account be full of money!" Or, they look at their old jalopy, decide they need a new car, and say, "In the name of Jesus I claim a new Monte Carlo in faith." Then, when they don't get what they "believed" for, they're sorely disappointed.

So many want the prize of faith, but aren't willing to run the race of faith. So many want to bear the fruit of the Spirit in their lives, but aren't willing to pay the price of discipleship. So many want God to answer their prayers, but aren't willing to pray in His will.

Faith in Christ is not a magic wand. Using the name of Jesus will not force God to give you what you want, especially if what you want is something God knows you don't need.

At the same time, the results of faith are not necessarily instantaneous. God is not a one-hour prayer processing service. Faith requires commitment.

Effective faith means believing in God's will, and persevering persistently over time.

When you bake a cake, you don't just shout at the ingredients, "Mix yourself and jump in the oven!" People would think you'd gone nuts if they heard you talking like that in your kitchen. And you would be. Nor do you take whatever ingredients you feel like using and just throw them together and hope you get a chocolate cake.

Either you've got a written recipe in front of you, or you've been taught by someone else how to bake a cake. Whether it's written out in front of you or in your head, you have a plan which you follow to prepare your cake. And that plan, or recipe, specifies exactly which ingredients you need. And using your own two hands, you mix and blend the ingredients.

God's Word is our plan for Christian living. His will is the prime ingredient list for how we live our life.

Finally, when all the proper ingredients are mixed according to the recipe, do you have a cake yet? No. You have the potential for a cake, but it will take more time and a lot of heat to actually become a cake.

So it is in our lives. When you become a Christian

and accept Christ into your life, you possess all you need
to become holy and mature in the Lord. But it's going
to take time and persistence. And probably a lot of heat!

God listened to Moses, and answered, "Now, you're
going to see My glory. And so is Pharaoh. The battle's
still going to be rough, but Pharaoh's going to get it."
God was waiting for a reason. He wanted to make sure
Pharaoh and the Egyptians fully understood exactly
Who they were dealing with. God wanted to illustrate
to them what He was all about.

The Egyptian culture was decadent. They served a
number of gods and idols. Even Pharaoh was considered
a god. The power of Satan had a strong grip on the entire nation. God knew that He needed to make it per-
fectly clear that He was not just another god, that He
was the one God. And He did.

It took a number of miraculous demonstrations, and
ten plagues but God got His message across in no uncer-
tain terms. Pharaoh and his people paid dearly, too. The
price of sin is always high. And the spiritual battle going
on here was especially bloody.

Finally, Pharaoh released the Israelites. They were
free at last. What a relief, right! Yes, it was a relief,
but their ordeal with Pharaoh still wasn't ended.

In Matthew, Jesus stated, "When an unclean spirit
goes out of a man, he goes through dry places, seeking
rest, and finds none. Then he says, 'I will return to my
house from which I came' " (Matthew 12:43-44). Just
because you've defeated Satan once doesn't mean you'll
never be bothered by him again. You've got to keep your
spiritual guard up continually. Whenever the Enemy

attacks, though, God is right there giving us strength to resist.

The Lord warned Moses and Moses was ready when Pharaoh changed his mind and started after the Israelites with his soldiers. And it was here that God performed what is probably His best-known miracle.

The children of Israel had come to a standstill on the banks of the Red Sea. They had no boats, and Pharaoh's army was bearing down on them. Did the Israelites use the weapon of praise? No, they did what they were best at — complained. But Moses had finally gotten with the program. He was beginning to understand what victorious living was all about.

Standing before the Israelites, "Moses said to the people, 'Do not be afraid. Stand still, and see the salvation of the Lord, which He will accomplish for you today. For the Egyptians whom you see today, you shall see again no more forever. The Lord will fight for you, and you shall hold your peace' " (Exodus 14:13-14).

Every principle of victorious Christian living we've discussed so far is evident in this situation. Except for one element — action! Moses was giving a stirring speech, and it was full of good stuff, yet it was time to move on. God broke in, and said, "Tell the children of Israel to go forward" (vs. 15).

Isn't this so typical of us? We run from seminar to seminar, and speaker to speaker. We go out and buy all the wonderful books and teaching tapes on faith, dynamic living, prosperity, learning God's will, and so on. Yet, we're so taken with learning all the principles, we never actually put them into practice.

Moses knew all the principles. And so did the Israel-ites. They'd seen God's power at work already in the signs and wonders and plagues that got them released in the first place. They didn't need more principles or teaching; they needed to step out in faith and get moving!

If they hadn't walked across the Red Sea that day, all the faith in the world wouldn't have saved them. They could have stood there staring at the divided waters and been slaughtered by the Egyptians. Are you like that? Has God provided the answer you need, yet you refuse to step out in faith and accept it? Many peo-ple, suffering from illness, would be healed if they'd step out in faith. Many people suffering from financial trouble would have their needs met, if they would step out in faith.

For some, healing may mean surgery. Yet, they refuse the surgery out of fear and doubt and confusion. If surgery is the answer, God will provide the money for your hospital bills and guide the hands of the surgeon as he operates. For others, the answer to financial prob-lems is taking a job they may not want, but could do. Take the job, earn the money you need now, and trust God to give you the job you want later.

The children of Israel stood in the presence of the supernatural as they watched the Red Sea part and the dry land appear. And they used their natural strength — their feet — to walk across to the other side.

These are the ingredients for victorious Christian liv-ing: one part natural, and one part supernatural. It takes both. God's miracles are made worthless when we refuse to step out in faith and accept them. God is depending on you to depend on Him.

God will never ask you to do something you can't. When He calls you to victory, as He has called each of us, He also equips us with all we need to achieve victory. We must listen for His will, act in obedience, persevere in faith, and use all that He has endowed us with. Sometimes, the miracle you need to turn your crisis into opportunity is right at your fingertips.

Like the popular bumper sticker slogan states, "God don't make junk!" He doesn't call you to leave you stranded. He won't take you to the edge of your promised land, and leave you. He will take you through if you will take His hand and go forward!

CHAPTER NINE

Seven Characteristics of Victory

Are you facing a battle right now? We're going to look at five biblical battles, and examine seven characteristics that are common in battle situations — even spiritual battles.

Our five example battles are the one we just looked at in the last chapter where Moses defeated Pharaoh (Exodus 14); the battle of Jericho (Joshua 6); the battle of Jehoshaphat against a multitude (2 Chronicles 20); David and Goliath (1 Samuel 17); and Gideon against the Midianites (Judges 7).

First, in each battle, the odds of winning seemed impossible. A prime example of this was the situation we just looked at concerning the children of Israel as they stood at the edge of the Red Sea. "That wasn't a battle!" you say. Then you weren't paying attention! Remember, we're fighting a spiritual war, not a war with flesh and blood people. Just because the children of

Israel were unarmed doesn't mean they weren't involved in warfare.

Let's look at the situation again as presented in Exodus 14. Here is poor Moses, a reluctant leader to begin with. Now, he has somewhere between three to six million people waiting for him to make some kind of executive decision, all grumbling at the same time. They've got their backs up against a wall — the Red Sea. And hot on their heels is the Egyptian army and a mob. Verses 6 and 7 read, "So he [Pharaoh] made ready his chariot and took his people with him. Also, he took six hundred choice chariots, and all the chariots of Egypt with captains over every one of them."

Just imagine the situation. The people weren't prepared for battle; they had just come out of servitude, and had spent the last several days in unusually hard labor. The children were hot and cranky. Everyone was loaded down with hastily packed loads of possessions. And they were all probably hungry and thirsty, and not a McDonald's in sight! Worse yet, there was no cavalry to rescue them!

The situation looked hopeless. But it wasn't. Neither is yours.

Moses looked to God for help and He was there. The waters parted and the people went across. Then, they stood on the other shore and watched the greatest show on earth!

Now, if I had been one of Pharaoh's army I would have had serious doubts about charging across the bottom of the Red Sea. Wouldn't you? I mean, this is an obvious miracle, at least worth a second glance. Yet, the army was so gripped with evil and hatred they ignored the miracle and recklessly plunged down the bank onto the sea bottom. Pharaoh and his horde were thirsty for blood. All they got was a big drink of the Red Sea!

To us, our problems seem insurmountable. To God, they're a piece of cake. We need to allow Him to open our spiritual eyes and see our problems as He does.

Second, the Lord always raised up a leader to deliver the people. Moses was a leader. In the battle of Jericho, Joshua was called. Against the Midianites, God raised up Gideon. To face a triple threat, God brought forth Jehoshaphat. And to destroy a single giant, God raised up a teenager.

In virtually each situation the men God chose to lead His people in the battle seemed very unlikely. In the natural they didn't appear to be qualified. But God sees beyond appearances. And, more important, God wanted to be glorified through these men in each situation.

God doesn't want us to become overly confident of our natural abilities. He wants us to depend upon Him. That's why He often chooses unlikely people for major tasks. When it happens to us, we have to throw ourselves on His mercy. We know He doesn't make mistakes, but still, we can't always see how He's going to use us.

When he went out to face Goliath, David didn't go on his own strength. He wasn't stupid or crazy. He knew that it was God in him that had allowed him to overcome the bears and lions he'd killed as they tried to destroy his flock. And he gave God the full credit. Even as he stood before the giant, David said, "I come to you in the name of the Lord of hosts . . . This day the Lord will deliver you into my hand . . . for the battle is the Lord's" (1 Samuel 17:45-47).

Notice David repeatedly stated that not he, little David, was going to kill Goliath — the Lord was going to do it. David was merely the tool God was using to bring Himself glory.

Are you facing trials? God is calling you to battle them in His name. Each of us can be "David" against our "Goliath" problems. God is calling you to victory.

Third, the victories were not immediate. As we saw with Moses, it took time and ten plagues to get the children of Israel out of Egypt. And after that, it took them forty years to get into their Promised Land. The Red Sea was only the first step in a long journey.

David didn't come out of nowhere. He'd been serving the Lord early on. He didn't start tackling bears and lions at age three, either. He didn't attain his level of faith overnight. And as with Moses, the victory over Goliath was David's first step. There would be other battles, and both victories and defeats, to follow.

And look at the battle of Jericho. Here is a study of supreme patience in what appears to be utter futility and foolishness.

Moses had just passed his authority on to Joshua before he died. And God had confirmed Joshua in his new position. The children of Israel had ended their wilderness wanderings and were ready to possess Canaan land. Their first obstacle was Jericho. What great military strategy, Joshua must have wondered, would God use? What great miracle would be seen? Joshua was in for a big surprise.

Using good military judgment, Joshua sends out spies. They report back, Joshua is encouraged, and he's ready to see fire fall from heaven or even something more wonderful. He's certain God will defeat Jericho for them.

He tells the people to prepare themselves and bring out the ark of the covenant. He says, "Sanctify yourselves, for tomorrow the Lord will do wonders among you" (Joshua 3:5). And they did see wonders. They crossed the Jordan in the same manner they had crossed the Red Sea. But that was nothing, thought Joshua, compared to what's going to happen to Jericho!

Then the Lord sent an angel to let Joshua in on His battle plan for Jericho. In Joshua 5:13-15, the encounter is recorded. Joshua saw the angel and drew his sword like a good soldier. Then, when he learned that it was the commander of the Lord's army he faced, he asked for his orders. What did the angel say? "Take off your sandals, Joshua. You're on holy ground."

The angel laid out the battle plan. The children of Israel were to march around the city blowing their rams' horns. And they were to do it for seven days! Can you imagine Joshua's dismay? He was a military man. And he'd seen the army of Pharaoh wiped out in an instant. Where was the fire from heaven? Where was the immediate, instantaneous defeat?

The defeat of Jericho came. But it took seven days of doing exactly what God commanded to be done to do it. Had Joshua tried to take the city on his own the first day he would have been dismally defeated. He had to wait in God's time.

This is important to keep in mind. The victory is ours, but it comes in time. If your victory comes in seven days, that's great. But don't forget, the Israelites had already waited forty years! So it actually took longer than a week.

The time it takes to win a victory isn't as important as how we spend that time. Joshua obeyed God's command to the letter. He remained faithful and committed to God, even though his soldier's instinct wanted to act more quickly.

Use the time before your victory to get closer to God. Get more of God's Word into you. Use it to prepare yourself for the victory.

Fourth is that in each battle, there was the assurance that God was in the battle. God is on your side. He doesn't abandon us in the heat of battle. Satan wants to convince us that we're alone, and it may seem like we are. Friends may let you down, but God is always there.

Jehoshaphat faced three armies, and more, all at the same time. 2 Chronicles 20:1 states, "The people of Moab with the people of Ammon, and others with them besides the Ammonites, came to battle against Jehoshaphat."

What was Jehoshaphat's reaction when he heard the news? He feared, as any normal person would, and turned to the Lord, declaring a fast throughout Judah. God responded, and spoke through Jahaziel, who prophesied, "Do not be afraid nor dismayed because of this great multitude, for the battle is not yours, but God's" (vs. 15). Sound familiar?

In every situation when God's people came against an enemy, as long as they were in God's will, He was with them, and always gave them assurance of His presence. God is with you in all of your battles, too.

The fifth characteristic is related to the fourth, and is that the victory was always proclaimed by faith before the battles began.

Jehosphaphat not only received assurance in the words he heard, but it was the pronouncement of absolute victory. After all, if God is for you, who is going to be against you?

David stood in front of the mocking Philistine and told him, "Today, the Lord is going to use me to destroy you." He told the giant that he was as good as dead! David spoke his faith and then acted in faith.

As we've seen, God has promised us victory over all our problems in this life. We can have one hundred percent victory over each problem. The problems will never stop coming, but we are assured of victory over each one. In faith, knowing God has promised us His excellence, we must speak to adversity and tell it to be gone.

Fred Price told about a woman in his church who always stood up and testified every time they had testimonies. She had a huge tumor on her neck right where everyone could see it. Yet each time, every week, she stood up and proclaimed, "I thank God that by His stripes I am healed!"

Brother Price said this went on for an entire year. Each Sunday, she gave the same testimony, and the tumor was right there on her neck as plain as day.

But one day, she got up, and went to the mirror to brush her hair. She looked in the mirror and the tumor was gone! She knew she had the victory. She proclaimed her victory in faith. She stayed faithful and committed in the battle. She persisted in her faith. And she received the victory.

Sixth, all of these battles were spiritual battles. They all involved swords and armies, but they were all battles between God and the forces of hell.

Each battle contained an element of the supernatural combining with the natural to produce the victory. And they each represented major defeats for Satan's kingdom.

Satan uses armies just as he uses individuals. The Egyptians were a godless people, and Pharaoh had no use for God. The people Joshua destroyed were all spiritual heathen. They knew the power of God, and trembled at the approach of the children of Israel, yet still clung to their paganisms of idol worship and worse.

Goliath openly defied God and insulted His people, and his attitude was representative of the Philistines. The Moabites and Ammonites that came against Jehoshaphat worshipped a god called Molech. Their worship of this heathen god included temple prostitution and even child sacrifice.

The spiritual warfare still rages around us. Often we're oblivious to it, but it's there. The devil will use anyone and any means to destroy God's creation — you and me. This is why in each situation, we must remember the battle cry, "The battle is the Lord's." It's not ours.

The seventh and final characteristic is that the side God is on always wins. Seems pretty obvious, right? It should be, but we seem to forget it a lot.

Two things I've discovered about victories is that they don't always come when we expect, and they don't come the way we expect them. This means that the victory often isn't very obvious, so it's easy to forget that God is with us in the battle.

Gideon was preparing to go against the Midianites and he was gathering the people together into an army. He had a real large group when the Lord spoke to him. "And the Lord said to Gideon, 'The people who are with you are too many' " (Judges 7:2). God told Gideon to tell those who were afraid to go home. Twenty-two thousand left. Only ten thousand stayed.

Gideon lost more than two-thirds of his army. This totally went against military strategy. Yet, God wasn't through. He trimmed the ten thousand down to three hundred. Gideon had less than a tenth of his original army, and by natural standards, they were headed to a sure death. But — God was on their side!

We plead to God, "Give us ten thousand dollars to meet our debts." And God gives us one thousand dollars. As we look at the situation, it's hopeless. But, we're forgetting Who's on our side. If we need ten thousand dollars and God gives us one thousand dollars — He's going to meet the need with the thousand, or provide the rest when we need it!

Gideon took his three-hundred-man army and defeated the Midianites using pitchers, torches, and trumpets!

When God is on your side, you don't need a dozen college degrees, fancy technology, or high social status to win your victories. All you need is what God has given you.

Even though the outcome looks impossible, and the odds are against you, if God is on your side, you will have victory. Even though you feel inadequate for the task, or have been in the battle for a long time, if God is on your side, the victory is yours. God's Word promises victory to His people. Proclaim your victory in faith, walk committed to the Lord, and the battle will be won.

Look the devil in the eye, tell him you're not quitting, that you're not going to be defeated anymore, that you've got God on your side, and you're a winner!

CHAPTER TEN

Stepping Into Victory

Are you ready for victory in your life? Do you want God's excellence in your daily walk? Whatever your problem, whatever your need, victory can be yours.

Paul declares in 1 Corinthians 15:57, "But thanks be to God, who gives us the victory through our Lord Jesus Christ." It is God's will for every Christian to live a victorious life. He doesn't want you defeated. He wants you strong and experiencing daily spiritual success.

In the next verse, Paul tells us a little more about how to keep the victory. He says, "Therefore, my beloved brethren, be steadfast, immovable, always abounding in the work of the Lord, knowing that your labor is not in vain" (vs. 58). These are the capstones to victory.

If you want victory, and when you get it you want to keep it, you've got to live a consistent Christian life.

The devil is consistent in his persistence to get you down. You can't defeat him if you're living a part-time faith.

Satan will attack you relentlessly, day in and day out, for years, in the same area of your weakness. You must counterattack by determining to bring that weakness under the blood of Christ every day, for as long as it takes.

Paul says be steadfast and immovable! That means you have to stick to it. Be steadfast, not bedfast! Even when you don't feel as though you can go on, go on anyway. Victory comes by not quitting.

What would happen if every morning you decided you were too tired to get up for work? You'd lose your job. You wouldn't have any income. Your utilities would be cut off, and soon you'd starve to death.

That's what will happen if you give up the battle before you win the victory. Defeat in one area of your life leads to defeat in others. You've got to hang tough, or get hanged.

As athletes say, no pain no gain. Serving the Lord takes effort and diligence. It takes determination. When you don't feel like praying, you've got to decide to pray anyway. When you don't feel like reading the Bible, read it anyway. You know you need it, so read it.

God honors your effort. When you're tired and you still remain faithful, He'll renew you. He'll lift you up and give you the strength you need.

When God says it's time to go into battle, you must set your goal before you and head toward it. And when you can't move, you become immovable. Don't let the

Enemy push you back. Hold your ground, and then push on.

Paul also says to "abound in the work of the Lord." What does this mean? Keep busy for God! Get involved in ministry in your church. Study your Bible daily. Witness to your friends and neighbors. Pray for missionaries and loved ones. Take meals to the elderly shut-ins. Help take care of the church buildings. Teach a Sunday School class.

The point is that when you're involved in the things of God, you won't be so easily distracted by the things of the world.

Plus, being active affects your attitude. You feel better about yourself. You feel useful and wanted. You feel more comfortable around others, and are more readily drawn into fellowship. And helping others helps you focus away from your own problems.

Developing a strong sense of compassion for others is a good way to move into victory yourself. As you see others in need, you become more grateful for what you have, even if it's not much. And as you see God bless others it becomes easier to believe for your needs being met.

Watching God work in the lives of others, you'll be more ready to praise and rejoice, even in the midst of conflict. Victory comes more easily when you have the right attitude of praise.

God responds to a thankful, praising heart. Philippians 4:6 states, "Be anxious for nothing, but in everything by prayer and supplication, with thanksgiving, let your requests be made known to God." Tell

God your needs and desires, but do it with a grateful attitude.

Expect an answer, and praise God for it. If you are praying in God's will, the answer's on the way.

What if your answer doesn't come for twenty-five years? Keep praying, praising, and believing without wavering. Wouldn't you rather give God twenty-five years of praise than twenty-five years of doubt and complaining?

When you accepted Christ you became an overcomer. Look at 1 John 5. Verse 1 says that if you believe that Jesus is the Christ, you are born of God. Verse 4 says everyone who is born of God overcomes the world. "And this is the victory that has overcome the world — our faith. Who is he who overcomes the world, but he who believes that Jesus is the Son of God?"

You have within you the power and potential to overcome your problems. You've been equipped with everything you need to live a victorious Christian life.

Are you ready to receive your victory? Are you committed steadfastly to Jesus Christ? Are you willing to pay the cost of discipleship? Are you walking in God's will? Are you believing consistently for your answer to prayer? Are you praising God in your situation and thanking Him for all He's provided to you?

Then, what are you waiting for? Step out in victory and let God part your "Red Sea" of trouble before you. Walk across and begin possessing your promised land!